Collins
TERNATIONAL
RIMARY
NGLISH

Teacher's Guide 5

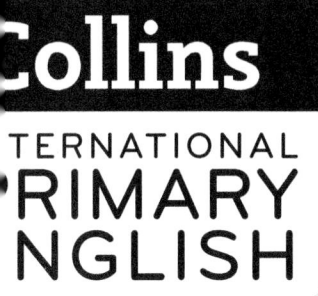

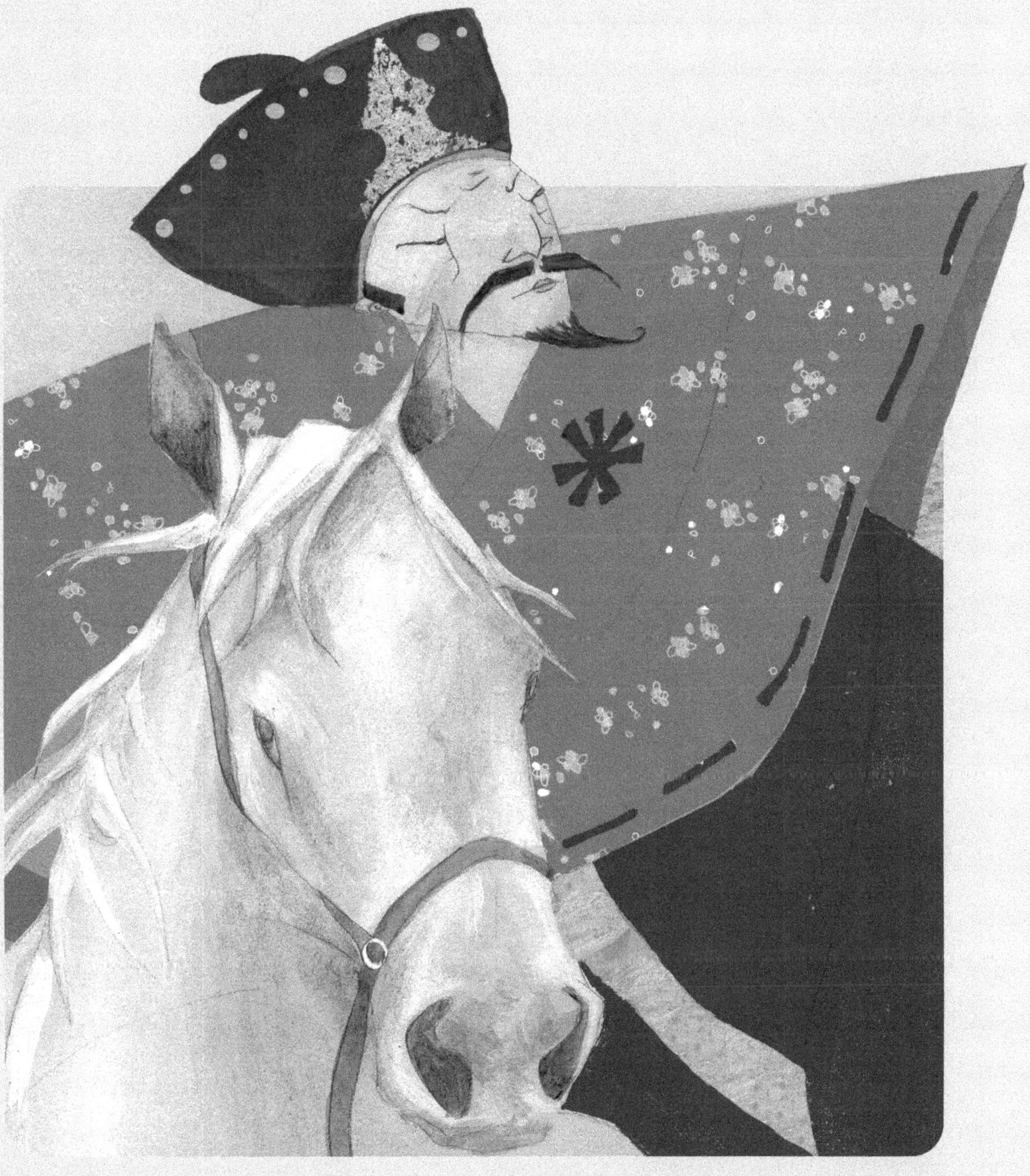

William Collins' dream of knowledge for all began with the publication of his first book in 1819.
A self-educated mill worker, he not only enriched millions of lives, but also founded a flourishing publishing house. Today, staying true to this spirit, Collins books are packed with inspiration, innovation and practical expertise. They place you at the centre of a world of possibility and give you exactly what you need to explore it.

Collins. Freedom to teach.

An imprint of HarperCollinsPublishers
The News Building
1 London Bridge Street
London SE1 9GF

Browse the complete Collins catalogue at
www.collins.co.uk

© HarperCollins*Publishers* Limited 2016

10 9 8 7

ISBN 978-0-00-814768-6

Daphne Paizee asserts her moral rights to be identified as the author of this work.

All rights reserved. No part of this publication may be reproduced, stored in a retrieval system, or transmitted in any form by any means, electronic, mechanical, photocopying, recording or otherwise, without the prior written permission of the Publisher or a licence permitting restricted copying in the United Kingdom issues by the Copyright Licensing Agency Ltd., 90 Tottenham Court Road, London W1T 4LP.

British Library Cataloguing in Publication Data
A catalogue record for this publication is available from the British Library.

Publisher Celia Wigley
Publishing manager Karen Jamieson
Commissioning editor Lucy Cooper
Series editor Karen Morrison
Managing editor Caroline Green
Editor Amanda Redstone
Project managed by Emily Hooton and Karen Williams
Edited by Karen Williams
Proofread by Gaynor Spry
Cover design by Amparo Barrera
Cover artwork by Serena Curmi
Internal design by Ken Vail Graphic Design
Typesetting by Ken Vail Graphic Design and Contentra Technologies India Private Limited
Illustrations by Ken Vail Graphic Design, Advocate Art and Beehive Illustrations
Production by Robin Forrester

Printed and bound by CPI Group (UK) Ltd, Croydon, CR0 4YY

Contents

Section 1 Introduction

About Collins International Primary English — 5

Assessment in primary English — 6

Laying the foundations of learning to read in the early stages — 8

Dictation — 8

Learning objectives matching grid — 9

Section 2 Unit-by-Unit Support

Unit 1: Danger!
Unit overview — 18
Learning objectives — 18
Related resources — 19
Week 1 — 19
Week 2 — 22
Week 3 — 24

Unit 2: In the post
Unit overview — 28
Learning objectives — 28
Related resources — 29
Week 1 — 29
Week 2 — 30
Week 3 — 33

Unit 3: Bugs
Unit overview — 36
Learning objectives — 36
Related resources — 36
Week 1 — 37
Week 2 — 39
Week 3 — 40

Unit 4: At the library
Unit overview — 44
Learning objectives — 44
Related resources — 44
Week 1 — 45
Week 2 — 48
Week 3 — 50

Unit 5: Amazing journeys
    Unit overview   53
    Learning objectives   53
    Related resources   54
    Week 1   54
    Week 2   56
    Week 3   57

Unit 6: Myths and legends
    Unit overview   60
    Learning objectives   60
    Related resources   61
    Week 1   61
    Week 2   63
    Week 3   66

Unit 7: On stage
    Unit overview   69
    Learning objectives   69
    Related resources   69
    Week 1   70
    Week 2   72
    Week 3   75

Unit 8: Amazing ships
    Unit overview   77
    Learning objectives   77
    Related resources   78
    Week 1   78
    Week 2   80
    Week 3   81

Unit 9: Sights, sounds and feelings
    Unit overview   84
    Learning objectives   84
    Related resources   85
    Week 1   85
    Week 2   87
    Week 3   89

Section 3 Photocopiable masters (PCMs)

PCM 1–19   92

Formal assessment 1   111

Formal assessment 2   115

Formal assessment 3   120

Introduction

About Collins International Primary English

Collins International Primary English is specifically written to fully meet the requirements of the Cambridge Primary English curriculum framework, and the material has been carefully developed to meet the needs of primary English learners and teachers in a range of international contexts.

The material at each level has been organised into nine units, each based around particular text types. The activities in each unit are introduced and explored in contexts related to the selected texts.

The course materials are supplemented and enhanced by a range of print and electronic resources, including photocopiable (printable) master sheets for support, extension and assessment of classroom based activities (you can find these on pages 92 to 123 of this Teacher's Guide as well as on the digital resource) and a range of interactive digital activities to add interest and excitement to learning. Reading texts are supported by audio presentations.

Components of the course

For each of Stages 1–6 as detailed in the Cambridge Primary English curriculum framework, we offer:

- a full colour, highly illustrated Student's Book with integral reading texts
- a write-in Workbook linked to the Student's Book
- this ructions for using the materials
- an interaccomprehensive Teacher's Guide with clear insttive digital package, which includes warm-up presentations, audio files of readings, interactive activities and record keeping for teacher use only.

Approach

The course is designed with learner-centred learning at its heart. Learners work through a range of contextualised reading, writing, speaking and listening activities with guidance and support from their teacher. Plenty of opportunity is provided for the learners to consolidate and apply what they have learnt and to relate what they are learning both to other contexts and the environment in which they live.

Much of the learners' work is conducted in pairs or small groups in line with international best practice. The tasks and activities are designed to be engaging for the learners and to support teachers in their assessment of learner progress and achievement. Each set of lessons is planned to support clear learning objectives and the activities within each unit provide opportunities for oral and written feedback by the teacher as well as self- and peer-assessment options.

Throughout the course, there is a wide variety of learning experiences on offer. The materials are organised so that they do not impose a rigid structure, but rather allow for a range of options linked to the learning objectives.

Differentiation

Differentiation in the form of support and extension ideas is built into the unit-by-unit teaching support in this Teacher's Guide.

Achievement levels are likely to vary from learner to learner, so we have included a graded set of assessment criteria in each weekly review section. The square, circle and triangle coded assessment criteria indicate what learners at varying levels might be expected to have achieved each week. The square indicates what can be expected of almost all learners. The circle indicates what might be expected of most learners, and triangle indicates what level of achievement might be expected from more able learners. Levels will vary as some learners may find some topics more interesting and/or easier; similarly, some may excel at speaking activities rather than written ones.

Teacher's Guide

The Teacher's Guide offers detailed guidance for covering each unit. Each unit is designed to cover three teaching weeks. Teachers know their class and context best, so they should feel free to vary the pace and the amount of work covered each week to suit their circumstances. Each unit has a clear structure, with an introduction, suggestions for introducing the unit, learning objectives and a resource list of supporting materials that can be used in the unit.

Student's Book

The Student's Book offers a clear structure and easy-to-follow design to help learners to navigate the course. The following features are found at all levels:

- A range of fiction, non-fiction, poetry, playscripts and transactional texts are provided to use as a starting point for contextualised learning.
- Skills-based headers allow teachers to locate activities within the curriculum framework and indicate to learners what skills are being focussed on in each task.
- Clear instruction rubrics are provided for each activity. The rubrics allow learners to develop more and more independent learning as they begin to master and understand instructive text. The rubrics also model assessment type tasks and prepare Grammar and language boxes provide teaching text and examples to show the language feature in use. These are coloured so that learners can easily recognise them as they work through the course.
- The notepad feature contains reminders, hints and interesting facts.

Workbook

The Workbook is clearly linked to the Student's Book. The activities here contain structured spaces for the learners to record answers. The activities can be used as classroom tasks, for homework, or for assessment purposes. The completed Workbook tasks give the teacher an opportunity to check work and give written feedback and/or grades. The learners have a consolidated record of their work and parents can see what kind of activities the learners are doing in class.

Digital resources

The digital resources are offered online by subscription. You can access these at Collins Connect. These resources can be used to introduce topics and support learning and assessment.

The interactive activities include:

- drag-and-drop activities
- matching activities
- look-cover-say-spell activities
- cloze procedure (fill in the missing words)
- labelling diagrams
- and many more.

Learners receive instant feedback when they complete the activities and the responses are randomised so the learners can complete the tasks they enjoy more than once, getting a different arrangement of items each time.

Some materials can be printed out for use in the classroom. For example, there is an additional assessment task provided for each unit. This is in the form of a simple test. It can be printed and used in class or as a homework task. These tasks are teacher marked.

Collins Connect offers an easy and accessible method of keeping records. Teachers can compile class lists and keep track of progress in an easy-to-use and well-supported system.

Using the audio files in the classroom

All of the reading and listening texts in the course have been recorded and are supplied with the digital subscription as audio recordings. The audio recordings offer a range of voices, pace and expression and they will enhance the classroom experience by introducing variety and making it easier for the teacher to observe learners as they listen to, and follow texts. The audio files can also be accessed in the student-only view so learners who are struggling with reading can listen to these on their own as many times as they like.

We suggest that you use the audio recordings as you introduce each reading text. Learners can either listen only or follow in their books as they listen to the text. Following and listening allows them to hear the words and the correct pronunciation and also to get a sense of where to pause, where to change expression and how to pace themselves when they are reading aloud.

Assessment in primary English

In the primary English programme, assessment is a continuous, planned process that involves collecting information about learner progress and learning in order to provide constructive feedback to both learners and parents and also to guide planning and the next teaching steps.

The Cambridge Primary English curriculum framework makes it clear what the learners are expected to learn and achieve at each level. Our task as teachers is to assess whether or not the learners have achieved the stated goals using clearly-focussed, varied, reliable and flexible methods of assessment.

In the Collins International Primary English course, assessment is continuous and in-built. It applies the principles of international best practice and ensures that assessment:

- is ongoing and regular
- supports individual achievement and allows for learners to reflect on their learning and set targets for themselves
- provides feedback and encouragement to the learners
- allows for integration of assessment into the activities and classroom teaching by combining different assessment methods, including observations, questioning, self-assessment and formal and informal tasks/tests
- uses strategies that cater for a variety of learner needs in the classroom (language, physical, emotional and cultural), and acknowledges that the learners do not all need to be assessed at the same time, or in the same way
- allows for, and prepares learners for, more formal summative assessment including controlled activities, tasks and tests.

Formal written assessment

The Collins International Primary English course offers a set of assessment sheets that teachers can use to assess learning formally and to award marks if necessary. These sheets test the skills and competencies developed in a cumulative manner. In some cases, learners will use the same texts as context; in other cases, they will be expected to read and make sense of an unseen text and to answer a range of contextualised questions based on that.

At Stage 3, there is a formal assessment task (test) at the end of units 3, 6 and 9.

In addition to the materials supplied in the course, schools may opt for their learners to take standardised Cambridge Primary progression tests at Stages 3, 4, 5 and 6. These tests are developed by Cambridge Assessment International Education but they are written and marked in schools. Teachers download tests and administer them in their own classrooms. Cambridge International provides a mark scheme and you can upload learners' test results and then analyse the results and print reports. You can also compare a learner's results against their class, school or other schools around the world and on a year-by-year basis.

Laying the foundations of learning to read in the early stages

To learn to read and write, children need to be phonologically aware and have a functional understanding of the alphabet along with an understanding of the purpose and value of print. Successful reading and writing depends on their ability to make the association between all three of these skills.

Learning to read should be treated as an enjoyable problem-solving activity. Children must be encouraged to use a wide range of strategies to help them to read unknown words.

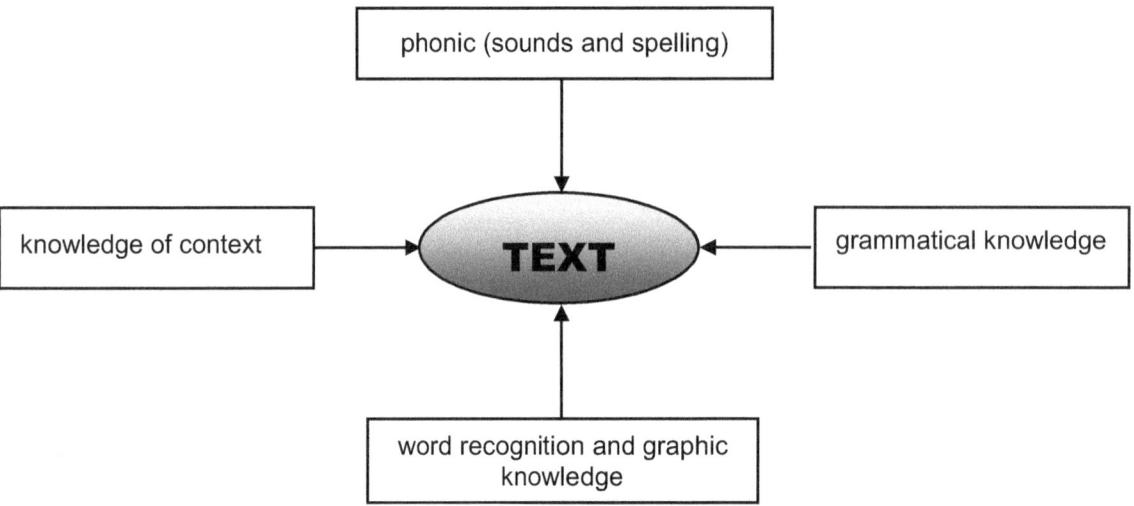

Dictation

In this stage, learners need to be able to write simple sentences, dictated by the teacher, from memory (3W07). This serves to reinforce basic spelling rules, consolidate work on writing sentences, and also gives learners a chance to practise and improve their handwriting skills.

You should give the class a dictation task at least once per week. Use the spelling words and sentence structures that you have taught during that week and make up simple sentences. Two or three sentences at a time are sufficient at this level. Ask the learners to put their pencils down and listen while you read the sentence slowly and clearly. Read it again and then ask them to write it from memory.

Learning objectives matching grid

The types of reading texts and the objectives covered in each unit are listed here by strand for easy reference. These same objectives are listed at the beginning of each unit in the unit-by-unit support section of this guide.

Unit 1	Reading	Writing	Listening and speaking
Danger! Texts: *The Rescue* (adventure story) *A busy day for firefighters* (non-fiction report) Listening text: *Instructions*	3Rx1 Answer questions with some reference to single points in a text; 3 Rx2 Scan a passage to find specific information and answer questions; 3Rx3 Identify the main points or gist of a text; 3R01 Use effective strategies to tackle blending unfamiliar words to read, including sounding out, separating into syllables, using analogy, identifying known suffixes and prefixes, using context; 3R05 Read aloud with expression to engage the listener; 3R07 Use knowledge of punctuation and grammar to read age-appropriate texts with fluency, understanding and expression; 3Rw2 Consider words that make an impact, e.g. adjectives and powerful verbs.	3W07 Write simple sentences, dictated by the teacher, from memory; 3Wa2 Write portraits of characters; 3Wa7 Write first-person accounts and descriptions based on observation; 3Wp6 Learn the basic conventions of speech punctuation and begin to use speech marks; 3Wp8 Collect examples of nouns, verbs and adjectives, and use the terms appropriately; 3Ws1 Use effective strategies to tackle segmenting unfamiliar words to spell, including segmenting into individual sounds, separating into syllables, using analogy, identifying known suffixes and prefixes, applying known spelling rules, visual memory, mnemonics; 3Ws3 Learn rules of adding –ing, –ed, –s to verbs; 3W05 Identify misspelt words and keep individual spelling log; 3Wa1 Develop descriptions of settings in stories; 3Wa4 Explore vocabulary for introducing and concluding dialogue, e.g. 'said', 'asked';	3SL3 Take turns in discussion, building on what others have said; 3SL4 Listen and respond appropriately to others' views and opinions; 3SL5 Listen and remember a sequence of instructions; 3SL8 Develop sensitivity to ways that others express meaning in their talk and non-verbal communication.

		3Wa8 Write book reviews summarising what a book is about; 3 Wp10 Understand that verbs are necessary for meaning in a sentence; 3 Wp12 Know irregular forms of common verbs;	
Unit 2	**Reading**	**Writing**	**Listening and speaking**
In the post Texts: *Postcards, formal and informal letters, notes, emails*	3R09 Use IT sources to locate simple information; 3Rv1 Identify the main purpose of a text; 3Rx1 Answer questions with some reference to single points in a text; 3Rx3 Identify the main points or gist of a text; 3Rw3 Consider ways that information is set out on a page and on a screen, e.g. lists, charts, bullet points.	3W07 Write simple sentences, dictated by the teacher, from memory; 3W10 Make a record of information drawn from a text, e.g. by completing a chart; 3W09 Use a dictionary or electronic means to find the spelling and meaning of words; 3Wp5 Recognise the use of the apostrophe to mark omission in shortened words, e.g. 'can't', 'don't'; 3Wp9 Identify pronouns and understand their function in a sentence; 3Wp12 Know irregular forms of common verbs; 3Wp13 Ensure grammatical agreement of pronouns and verbs in using standard English; 3Wa6 Establish purpose for writing, using features and style based on model texts; 3Wa10 Write letters, notes and messages; 3Ws2 Explore words that have the same spelling but different meanings (homonyms), e.g. 'form', 'wave'. 3Ws6 Organise words or information alphabetically using first two letters.	3SL1 Speak clearly and confidently in a range of contexts, including longer speaking turns; 3SL3 Take turns in discussion, building on what others have said; 3SL4 Listen and respond appropriately to others' views and opinions.

Unit 3	Reading	Writing	Listening and speaking
Bugs Texts: *Bugs* (extended rhyming poem) *Germs* (non-fiction text) Listening text: *Instructions for washing hands* Listening text: *How flies spread disease*	3R01 Use effective strategies to tackle blending unfamiliar words to read, including sounding out, separating into syllables, using analogy, identifying known suffixes and prefixes, using context; 3Rv1 Identifying the main purpose of a text; 3Rv2 Understand and use the terms 'fact', 'fiction' and 'non-fiction'; 3Rx1 Answer questions with some reference to single points in text; 3Rx3 Identify the main points or gist of a text; 3R04 Practise learning and reciting poems; 3R05 Read aloud with expression to engage the listener; 3R07 Use knowledge of punctuation and grammar to read age-appropriate texts with fluency, understanding and expression.	3W05 Identify misspelt words in own writing and keep individual spelling logs; 3W07 Write simple sentences, dictated by the teacher, from memory; 3W09 Use a dictionary or electronic means to find the spelling and meaning of words; 3W10 Make a record of information drawn from a text, e.g. by completing a chart; 3Wp8 Collect examples of nouns, verbs, adjectives, and use the terms appropriately; 3Wa5 Generate synonyms for high frequency words, e.g. 'big', 'little', 'good'; 3Wa9 Write and perform poems, attending to the sound of words; 3Wp1 Maintain accurate use of capital letters and full stops in showing sentences and check by reading own writing aloud; 3Ws1 Use effective strategies to tackle segmenting unfamiliar words to spell, including segmenting into individual sounds, separating into syllables, using analogy, identifying known suffixes and prefixes, applying known spelling rules, visual memory, mnemonics; 3Ws5 Use and spell compound words.	3SL3 Take turns in discussion, building on what others have said; 3SL4 Listen and respond appropriately to others' views and opinions; 3SL5 Listen and remember a sequence of instructions.

Unit 4	Reading	Writing	Listening and speaking
At the library Texts: *The Dewey decimal system* (non-fiction text) *Oranges in No Man's Land* (book review) *The Grand Plan to Fix Everything* (book review) *Elizabeth Laird* (information text) *Bookworms* (poem)	3R02 Read a range of story, poetry and information books and begin to make links between them; 3R03 Read and comment on books by the same author; 3R05 Read aloud with expression and engage the listener; 3R06 Sustain the reading of 48–64 page books, noting how a text is organised into sections or chapters; 3R09 Use IT sources to locate simple information; 3R11 Locate books by classification; 3Ri2 Infer the meaning of unknown words from context; 3Rw1 Consider how choice words can heighten meaning; 3Rv1 Identify the main purpose of a text; 3Rv2 Understand and use the terms 'fact' and 'non-fiction'; 3Rv3 Identify different types of stories and typical story themes.	3W07 Write simple sentences, dictated by the teacher, from memory; 3W10 Make a record of information drawn from text, e.g. by completing a chart; 3Wa5 Generate synonyms for high frequency words, e.g. 'big', 'little', 'good'; 3Wa8 Write book reviews summarising what a book is about; 3Wa10 Write letters, notes and messages; 3Wp2 Use a wider variety of sentence types including simple, compound and some complex sentences; 3Wp4 Vary sentence openings, e.g. with adverbials; 3Wp9 Identify pronouns and understand their function in a sentence; 3Wp10 Understand that verbs are necessary for meaning in a sentence; 3Wp11 Understand pluralisation and use the terms 'singular' and 'plural'; 3Wp13 Ensure grammatical agreement of pronouns and verbs in using standard English; 3Ws1 Use effective strategies to tackle segmenting unfamiliar words to spell, including segmenting into individual sounds, separating into syllables, using analogy, identifying known suffixes and prefixes, applying known spelling rules, visual memory, mnemonics.	3SL1 Speak clearly and confidently in a range of contexts, including longer speaking turns; 3SL3 Take turns in discussion, building on what others have said; 3SL6 Practise to improve performance when reading aloud.

Unit 5	Reading	Writing	Listening and speaking
Amazing journeys Texts: *The Journey of Humpback Whales* (non-fiction text including contents page and index) Listening text: *Cuckoos* *Captain Scott: Journey to the South Pole* (true adventure story)	3R01 Use effective strategies to tackle blending unfamiliar words to read, including sounding out, separating into syllables, using analogy, identifying known suffixes and prefixes, using context; 3R05 Read aloud with expression to engage the listener; 3R08 Locate information in a non-fiction text using a contents page and index; 3Rx1 Answer questions with some reference to single points in a text; 3R09 Use IT sources to locate simple information; 3R11 Locate books by classification; 3Rx2 Scan a passage to find specific information and answer questions; 3Ri1 Begin to infer meanings beyond the literal, e.g. about motives and character; 3Ri2 Infer the meaning of unknown words from the context; 3Rw3 Consider the way that information is set out on a page and on a screen, e.g. lists, charts, bullet points; 3Rv1 Identify the main purpose of a text.	3W04 Use IT to write, edit and present work; 3W07 Write simple sentences, dictated by the teacher, from memory; 3W10 Make a record of information drawn from a text, e.g. by completing a chart; 3Wa6 Establish purpose for writing, using features and style based on model texts; 3Wt2 Begin to organise writing in sections or paragraphs in extended stories; 3Wt3 Plan main points as a structure for story writing; 3Wp1 Maintain accurate use of capital letters and full stops in showing sentences and check by reading own writing aloud; 3Ws3 Learn rules of adding –ing, –ed, –s to verbs; 3WP9 Identify pronouns and understand their function in a sentence; 3Wp11 Understand pluralisation and use the terms 'singular' and 'plural'; 3Ws1 Use effective strategies to tackle segmenting unfamiliar words to spell, including segmenting into individual sounds, separating into syllables, using analogy, identifying known suffixes and prefixes, applying known spelling rules, visual memory, mnemonics. 3Ws4 Extend earlier work on prefixes and suffixes.	3SL2 Adapt tone of voice, use vocabulary and non-verbal features for different audiences; 3SL6 Practise to improve performance when reading aloud; 3SL7 Begin to adapt movement to create a character in drama.

Unit 6	Reading	Writing	Listening and speaking
Myths and legends Texts: *Tiddalik the Frog* (myth from Australia) *The Legend of Achilles* (legend from Ancient Greece) *The Legend of the Queen of Sheba* (legend from Africa) *The Wind and the Sun* (myth from Ghana)	3R01 Use effective strategies to tackle blending unfamiliar words to read, including sounding out, separating into syllables, using analogy, identifying known suffixes and prefixes, using context; 3R02 Read a range of story, poetry and information books and begin to make links between them; 3R06 Sustain the reading of 48–64 page books, noting how a text is organised into sections or chapters; 3R07 Use knowledge of punctuation and grammar to read age-appropriate texts with fluency, understanding and expression; 3R09 Use IT sources to locate simple information; 3R12 Read playscripts and dialogue, with awareness of different voices; 3Rx1 Answer questions with some reference to single points in a text; 3Rx2 Scan a passage to find specific information and answer questions; 3Rx3 Identify the main points or gist of a text; 3Rv3 Identify different types of stories and typical story themes; 3Ri1 Begin to infer meanings beyond the literal, e.g. about motives and character.	3W06 Use reading as a model for writing dialogue; 3W07 Write simple sentences, dictated by the teacher, from memory; 3W08 Write simple playscripts based on reading; 3Wa1 Develop descriptions of settings in stories; 3Wa4 Explore vocabulary for introducing and concluding dialogue, e.g. 'said', 'asked'; 3Wa5 Generate synonyms for high frequency words, e.g. 'big', 'little', 'good'; 3Wa6 Establish purpose for writing, using features and style based on model texts; 3Wa7 Write first-person accounts and descriptions based on observation; 3Wt1 Develop range of adverbials to signal the relationship between events; Continue to improve consistency in the use of tenses; 3Wt2 Begin to organise writing in sections or paragraphs in extended stories; 3Wt3 Plan main points as a structure for story writing; 3Wp6 Learn the basic conventions of speech punctuation and begin to use speech marks; 3Wp12 Know irregular forms of common verbs.	3SL3 Take turns in discussion, building on what others have said; 3SL4 Listen and respond appropriately to others' views and opinions; 3SL6 Practise to improve performance when reading aloud; 3SL7 Begin to adapt movement to create a character in drama.

Unit 7	Reading	Writing	Listening and speaking
On stage Texts: Listening text: *Chicken Licken* (traditional story) *Going … Going …* (playscript from southern Africa) *The Stone Cutter* (traditional tale from China, retold in poem form)	3R02 Read a range of story, poetry and information books and begin to make links between them; 3R05 Read aloud with expression to engage the listener; 3R10 Read and follow instructions to carry out an activity; 3R12 Read playscripts and dialogue, with awareness of different voices; 3Rx3 Identify the main points or gist of a text; 3Ri2 Infer the meaning of unknown words from the context; 3Rw2 Consider words that make an impact e.g. adjectives and powerful verbs.	3W07 Write simple sentences, dictated by the teacher, from memory; 3Wa10 Write letters, notes and messages; 3Wa2 Write portraits of characters; 3Wa3 Choose and compare words to strengthen the impact of writing, including noun phrases; 3Wa4 Explore vocabulary for introducing and concluding dialogue, e.g. 'said', 'asked'; 3Wa6 Establish purpose for writing, using features and style based on model texts; 3Wp5 Recognise the use of the apostrophe to mark omission in shortened words, e.g.' can't', 'don't'; 3Wp8 Collect examples of nouns, verbs, and adjectives, and use the terms appropriately.	3SL1 Speak clearly and confidently in a range of contexts, including longer speaking turns; 3SL2 Adapt tone of voice, use of vocabulary and non-verbal features for different audiences; 3SL6 Practise to improve performance when reading aloud; 3SL7 Begin to adapt movement to create a character in drama.
Unit 8	**Reading**	**Writing**	**Listening and speaking**
Amazing ships Texts: *The Titanic* (non-fiction text including contents page and index) *LNG Tankers* (information text with diagrams)	3R01 Use effective strategies to tackle blending unfamiliar words to read, including sounding out, separating into syllables, using analogy, identifying known suffixes and prefixes, using context; 3R02 Read a range of story, poetry, and information books and begin to make links between them; 3R07 Use knowledge of punctuation and	3W05 Identify misspelt words in own writing and keep individual spelling logs; 3W07 Write simple sentences, dictated by the teacher, from memory; 3W08 Write simple playscripts based on reading; 3W10 Make a record of information drawn from a text, e.g. by completing a chart;	3SL3 Take turns in discussion, building on what others have said; 3SL4 Listen and respond appropriately to others' view and opinions; 3SL8 Develop sensitivity to ways that others express meaning in their talk and non-verbal communication.

	grammar to read age-appropriate texts with fluency, understanding and expression; 3R08 Locate information in a non-fiction text using a contents page and index; 3R09 Use IT sources to locate simple information; 3Rw3 Consider ways that information is set out on a page and on a screen, e.g. lists, charts, bullet points; 3Rx2 Scan a passage to find specific information and answer questions; 3Ri1 Begin to infer meanings beyond the literal, e.g. about motives and character; 3Ri2 Infer the meaning of unknown words from the context.	3Wa1 Develop descriptions of settings in stories; 3Wa3 Choose and compare words to strengthen the impact of writing, including noun phrases; 3Wa7 Write first-person accounts and descriptions based on observation; 3Wp1 Maintain accurate use of capital letters and full stops in showing sentences and check by reading own writing aloud; 3Wp4 Vary sentence openings, e.g. with adverbials; 3Wp7 Use question marks, exclamation marks and commas in lists; 3Wp8 Collect examples of nouns, verbs and adjectives and use the terms appropriately; 3Wp12 Know irregular forms of common verbs; 3Ws1 Use effective strategies to tackle segmenting unfamiliar words to spell, including segmenting into individual sounds, separating into syllables, using analogy, identifying known suffixes and prefixes, applying known spelling rules, visual memory, mnemonics; 3Ws5 Use and spell compound words.	
Unit 9	**Reading**	**Writing**	**Listening and speaking**
Sights, sounds and feelings *A limerick* (limerick)	3R01 Use effective strategies to tackle blending unfamiliar words to read, including sounding out, separating into	3W07 Write simple sentences, dictated by the teacher, from memory; 3Wa5 Generate synonyms for high	3SL1 Speak clearly and confidently in a range of contexts, including longer speaking turns; 3SL4 Listen and respond appropriately to

Spaghetti (calligram) *I am Indira* (acrostic poem) *Riddle* (rhyming poem) *Teacher said …* (structured poem) *Ice Cream and Fizzy Lemonade* (rhyming poem) *Hurricane* (structured poem) *The Hen* (rhyming poem) *I Don't Know What To Do Today* (rhyming poem)	syllables, using analogy, identifying known suffixes and prefixes, using context; 3R02 Read a range of story, poetry and information books and begin to make links between them; 3R03 Read and comment on different books by the same author; 3R04 Practise learning and reciting poems; 3R05 Read aloud with expression to engage the listener; 3R07 Use knowledge of punctuation and grammar to read age-appropriate texts with fluency, understanding and expression; 3R09 Use IT sources to locate simple information; 3Rw1 Consider how choice of words can heighten meaning; 3Rw2 Consider words that make an impact, e.g. adjectives and powerful verbs; 3Ri1 Begin to infer meanings beyond the literal, e.g. about motives and character; 3Ri2 Infer the meaning of unknown words from the context; 3Rx2 Scan a passage to find specific information and answer questions.	frequency words, e.g. 'big', 'little', 'good'; 3Wa9 Write and perform poems, attending to the sound of words; 3Wp8 Collect examples of nouns, verbs and adjectives, and use the terms appropriately.	others' views and opinions; 3SL6 Practise to improve performance when reading aloud.

Note that handwriting is not taught explicitly in this course although objectives '3W01 Ensure consistency in the size and proportion of letters and the spacing of words', '3W02 Practise joining letters in handwriting', and '3W03 Build up handwriting speed, fluency and legibility' are implicitly covered in the activities and supporting notes in the Teacher's Guide. We recommend that teachers choose a structured and suitable course for teaching handwriting skills at Stage 3 level. *Collins Primary Focus: Handwriting* by Sue Peet, is a useful resource for this as the series progresses from the introduction of fine motor movements, through pre-cursive and cursive styles at the early stages, progressing to different handwriting styles, calligraphy and links to computer fonts at the higher levels.

Unit 1 Danger!

Unit overview

At the start of the year, it is always a good idea to get to know the different ability levels of your class, such as their reading ability and speaking confidence. In the first week the focus is mainly on reading and parts of speech. The second week allows the learners to discover how words make a story or sentence interesting. Verbs are discussed and the rule when using irregular verbs. In the third week the focus is on writing. Learners will use the knowledge gained from the first two weeks to help them to write interesting and descriptive sentences. There is a brief look at speech marks too.

Your classroom should be visually stimulating and also a form of reference for the learners. Spelling and grammar rules should be displayed as they are covered throughout the year. The learners must be encouraged and shown how to use real dictionaries and they should keep a personal dictionary in an exercise book. They will add words to it throughout the year. Words and pictures relevant to the unit's topic should be displayed.

Reading	Writing	Listening and speaking
3Rx1 Answer questions with some reference to single points in a text;	3W07 Write simple sentences, dictated by the teacher, from memory;	3SL3 Take turns in discussion, building on what others have said;
3 Rx2 Scan a passage to find specific information and answer questions;	3Wa2 Write portraits of characters;	3SL4 Listen and respond appropriately to others' views and opinions;
3Rx3 Identify the main points or gist of a text;	3Wa7 Write first-person accounts and descriptions based on observation;	3SL5 Listen and remember a sequence of instructions;
3R01 Use effective strategies to tackle blending unfamiliar words to read, including sounding out, separating into syllables, using analogy, identifying known suffixes and prefixes, using context;	3Wp6 Learn the basic conventions of speech punctuation and begin to use speech marks;	3SL8 Develop sensitivity to ways that others express meaning in their talk and non-verbal communication.
3R05 Read aloud with expression to engage the listener;	3Wp8 Collect examples of nouns, verbs and adjectives, and use the terms appropriately;	
3R07 Use knowledge of punctuation and grammar to read age-appropriate texts with fluency, understanding and expression;	3Ws1 Use effective strategies to tackle segmenting unfamiliar words to spell, including segmenting into individual sounds, separating into syllables, using analogy, identifying known suffixes and prefixes, applying known spelling rules, visual memory, mnemonics;	
3Rw2 Consider words that make an impact, e.g. adjectives and powerful verbs.	3Ws3 Learn rules of adding –ing, –ed, –s to verbs;	
	3W05 Identify misspelt words and keep individual spelling log;	
	3Wa1 Develop descriptions of settings in stories;	
	3Wa4 Explore vocabulary for introducing and concluding dialogue, e.g. 'said', 'asked';	
	3Wa8 Write book reviews summarising what a book is about;	
	3 Wp10 Understand that verbs are necessary for meaning in a sentence;	
	3 Wp12 Know irregular forms of common verbs.	

Related resources:

- Audio file: *The Rescue*
- Slideshow 1: Danger!
- PCM 1: *The Rescue* word search
- PCM 2: Book review
- PCM 3: Punctuation

Introducing the unit

Start the lesson by showing actual items or images of safety equipment such as: helmet, high visibility-vest (such as a traffic officer would wear), safety spectacles, international warning sign for electricity/voltage.

Ask the learners to name the items and to identify where, when and why these items are used. The learners ideally would respond that the items are worn for protection or to keep one safe. The discussion continues in order to work towards the response that some activities are dangerous, for example: rock/mountain climbing, motorcycling/cycling. Draw the learners' attention to the warning sign and ask what the sign tell us: be careful, watch out, danger. Have the word 'danger' written on card which will form part of the classroom display.

Give learners an opportunity to share any dangerous situations that they might have been in, or if they have seen something that is dangerous.

Display the word 'Danger' on a display board. Discuss the *g* in 'Danger'. Here, the *g* has a soft sound like *j* as in 'large', 'huge', 'giant'. Point out that sometimes *g* has a hard sound as in 'go'.

Week 1

Student's Book pages 1–5

Workbook page 1

Student's Book page 1

Listening and speaking

Ask the learners to look at the pictures and, in groups, to discuss the dangers they can see in the pictures. Draw the class together and share responses.

Writing

Nouns are the names of objects. Adjectives tell you more about nouns, e.g. the fluffy (adjective) cat (noun).

Ask learners to look at the pictures on page 1 again. Choose a specific picture and focus the learners' attention on it. Ask them to describe what they see. If the learners give simple answers such as: 'I see the ocean', prompt them, for example: Is the ocean deep or shallow? What is the weather doing? and so on. As the learners start calling out adjectives, write them on cards and pin them up below the 'danger' heading, for example: 'high', 'blazing', 'strong', 'terrified'. Explain that these words describe the noun. These words give you interesting information and make a story exciting. We call these words 'adjectives'.

1 Read through the sentences with the learners. Discuss some of the sentences with them, checking that they can distinguish between nouns and adjectives, before they write the sentences in their books.

Answers
a The workers were wearing hard hats.
b There was a huge fire on the mountain.
c The terrified boy was clinging to the rock on the mountain.
d There were big cars and small cars in the street.
e The metal ladder was against the wall of the house.
f A fierce thunderstorm struck the boat.

2 Ask learners to choose four pictures from page 1 and to write a sentence for each picture. Draw their attention to the adjectives that are on display in the classroom below the word 'Danger'. Maybe they can use some of them in their sentences. Read through the adjectives again.

Revise punctuation that must be used when writing a sentence, namely starting with a capital letter and ending the sentence with a full stop.

Support: Some learners really struggle to begin a sentence. You could either suggest a beginning or write a few beginnings on the board.

For example:

- On a very windy morning …
- We were walking down a steep hill …

Extension: If a learner has used a new adjective that does not appear on the display board, allow them to write it on a card and to pin it up.

Give learners a copy of PCM 1. This is a word search activity based on *The Rescue* which will help to consolidate nouns and adjectives.

Read through the words that are at the top of the page. Use this opportunity to revise nouns and adjectives, by asking after each word, 'Is this a noun or an adjective?' Explain to the learners that they must find these words in the grid. Tell them that the words can be written vertically, horizontally, straight across and diagonally. Write the first two rows of letters on the board and show the learners how to search for the words. When a word is found it should be circled on the grid and crossed out from the list at the top of the page.

Student's Book pages 2–4
Reading and speaking
1 Ask learners to look at the pictures on pages 2 and 3. Give them a few minutes to look at the pictures before asking the questions regarding the characters, setting and events of the story.

Talk to the learners about syllables and how they can them help to read a word. Do a few examples with the learners, for example: 'terrified' – terr/i/fied; 'rescue' – res/cue; 'harness' – har/ness.

2 The learners read the story *The Rescue* in pairs. Depending on the reading level of the class, it may be necessary to read the story to the learners first, followed by partnered reading. Move around the class listening to the reading, helping with difficult words where necessary. Help learners to read and understand words. They should sound out words and separate them into syllables and use the context to work out meanings. When everyone has finished reading the story, ask if there are any words that they do not understand and explain the meaning to them.

Support: It may be necessary to take a group of less able readers aside and assist them with the story.

Student's Book page 4
Reading and speaking
1 The learners answer the questions with their partner. When the majority of the class have completed the questions, discuss the answers with all the learners.

Answers
a Tom was walking along the cliff top.
b Tom was having a walk with his friend Alex.
c Tom was holding onto a narrow ledge.
d Tom heard a throb and a whirr.
e A man in a harness rescued Tom.
f The man put a belt around Tom's waist then he was pulled up into the helicopter.

Workbook page 1
Reading and understanding
The learners read the sentences and tick the sentences that are true about the story.

Answers
✓ Tom fell because his foot slipped and the ground fell away under him.
  Alex grabbed Tom's hand as he fell.
✓ Tom was clinging to the rock with his fingers.
  Tom was not afraid that he was going to fall down.
  Tom gave up and let go with his fingers and he fell down the cliff.
✓ The rescue helicopter pulled Tom off the cliff to safety.

Student's Book page 4
Reading and speaking
2 Read the story *The Rescue* with the learners again. In order to keep their attention, read a few paragraphs and then ask learners to read a few paragraphs.

Divide the learners into groups. Try to include a competent reader in each group. There are five questions, so ideally a group should have five learners and each learner should have a turn to read a question to the group.

Discuss the rules for working in groups:
- Everyone has a turn to speak.
- Respect the speaker.
- Encourage/help each other.

Encourage the learners to refer to the story for correct information. Circulate during the discussions, ensuring that each learner is involved in the activity. Control the time spent on each question by using a bell or clapping to signal time to move onto the next question. At the end of this exercise, there should be a consolidation of answers involving a class discussion. A way to avoid a repetition of answers is to write one word answers/phrases in a table on the board.

Answers
Answers could be recorded in a table:

a. Tom's feelings	b. Who called the helicopter?	c. Reasons why Tom was lucky	d. What would you do?	e. Did you enjoy the story? Why?
scared frightened anxious terrified panicky dizzy	Alex	Had a friend. Had a strong will. He was rescued. He grabbed hold of a ledge.	Shout! Hold on tightly.	Yes, it was exciting. It had a good ending.

Student's Book page 4

Speaking and writing

The learners work with a partner.

1 Ask: 'Who is the main character in the story *The Rescue*?' Ask: 'What do we know about Tom?' Read the questions in the Student's Book. Show the learners the adjectives that are in the box below the questions. Allow the learners sufficient time to do this activity. Walk around listening to the discussions. Afterwards, lead a class discussion on the character of Tom. Here again, have cards to hand to write down any adjectives that might come up. Add them next to the display of 'Danger'.

Answers
Answers will vary based on learners' perceptions and the opinions they have formed about Tom.

Workbook page 1

Reading and vocabulary

Tell the learners that they are going to complete a crossword puzzle. It may be the first time they've done a crossword puzzle, so take time to explain what must be done. Firstly, explain what is meant by 'clues'. Clues give you an idea of what the word might be. The crossword uses two words, namely 'across' and 'down'. These words tell you the direction in which you must write the word.

Answers
Across:

1 strong
3 tired
5 amazing
6 weak
Down:
2 terrified
4 safe

Student's Book page 5

Speaking and writing

2 Start with the whole class reading through the adjectives on display. The learners look at the pictures and discuss each character with their partner.

Answers
Answers will vary based on learners' perceptions and opinions.

3 For this activity, the learners work alone, using the previous discussion to help them to write a paragraph about one of the characters. Give the learners an idea of the length of the paragraph – five sentences would be the minimum. Give learners an opportunity to check their work for spelling mistakes. This would be a good time for learners to start their individual spelling logs for this year.

Support: Work with a group and help them to choose the adjectives that they could use for their paragraph.

Extension: The learners can underline the adjectives they used in their paragraph.

Weekly review

Use this rubric to assess learners' progress as they worked through the activities this week.

Level	Reading	Writing	Listening and speaking
■	This group reads at a slow pace, but still need some support to decode unfamiliar words.	This group is beginning to use capital letters and full stops when writing in sentences.	At times this group needs support to listen and requires prompting in order to respond appropriately.
●	This group is beginning to read with increased accuracy, mostly fluent and some expression.	This group can write in clear sentences using capital letters and full stops. They are beginning to use the past and present tenses with some accuracy.	This group demonstrates attentive listening. They listen carefully and respond appropriately.
▲	This group reads with accuracy, fluency and some expression, taking some notice of punctuation including speech marks.	This group can write in clear sentences using capital letters and full stops. They can use the past and present tenses accurately.	This group demonstrates attentive listening and engages with another speaker. They listen carefully and respond appropriately.

Week 2

Student's Book pages 5–7

Workbook pages 2–3

Student's Book page 5

Ask learners to perform the following actions: stand, hop, clap, sing, sit. Tell them that action words are called 'verbs'. Write the word 'verb' on a card and put it on the display board. Hand out a blank card to each learner and ask them to write an action word. This could also be done in groups. Pin up the words on the display board. Read them together, remove any that are not verbs and discuss why.

Workbook page 2

Vocabulary: verbs

Introduce the Workbook activity by asking the learners to name three actions that they can do, for example: 'eat', 'talk', 'play'.

Write 'bird' on the board. Ask the learners for three actions that a bird might do, for example: 'fly', 'tweet', 'rest'.

Ask the learners to open their Workbooks at page 2. They complete the activity by filling in three actions for each person/object.

Answers
Examples: Here are some answers, there are many more.
Alex: 'panic', 'run', 'shout'
Teacher: 'talks', 'writes', 'smiles'
Helicopter: 'flies', 'hovers', 'rotates'
Mother: 'cooks', 'fetches', 'works'

Student's Book page 5

Grammar: verbs

Read through the teaching text with the learners and discuss. The learners copy the sentences and underline the verb in each sentence.

Answers
a cried
b slid
c grabbed
d was clinging
e flew
f dangled
g felt
h was tired

Notepad feature:

Verbs have different forms. Read through the examples and discuss them with the learners.

Ask the learners to go back to the story *The Rescue*. Allow them a few minutes to find some verbs in the text that have a different form, for example: 'was shouting', 'been having'.

Workbook page 2

Grammar

Explain to the learners that they are going to read the sentences and underline the verbs. Remind them about verbs having different forms, for example: 'was running', 'am tired', 'are safe'.

Answers
a pulled
b was
c are
d Hold, shouted
e slid

Student's Book page 6
Listening and speaking
This is a group activity. Prepare enough sets of cards of verbs from *The Rescue* for each group, for example: 'treading air', 'stare', 'grin', 'dangle', 'cling', 'slip', 'spin', 'flap'. Show a set of cards to the learners and read them together. Divide the learners into groups. Give each group a set of cards and ask them to take turns to role-play an action for the rest of the group who must guess the action.

Spelling
Start the lesson by writing some sentences on the board, for example: 'I was look over the edge of the cliff.' 'I was cling on to the rock.'

Ask the learners to read the sentences and ask them to identify the verbs. Ask: 'Do the sentences sound correct? What needs to be changed?' The learners should identify the verbs and that *–ing* must be added. The learners complete the activity in the Student's Book.

Answers
telling, going, getting, swinging, playing, treading

Teach the spelling rule for irregular (short) vowels: double the last consonant before adding *–ing*.

Examples: sit – sitting; flap – flapping; drop – dropping; hug – hugging.

Workbook pages 2–3
Spelling
The learners have two activities to complete.

1 The first activity: circle the correct word to complete the sentence about *The Rescue*.

Answers
clinging; getting; telling; pulled

2 Remind the learners of the rule for irregular verbs: double the last consonant before adding *–ing*. The learners complete the activity by adding *–ing* to the verbs.

Answers
holding; getting; running; clinging; pulling; telling

Extension: The learners find more examples of irregular verbs and write them on cards for the display board.

Student's Book page 7
Vocabulary
Introduce the topic by repeating a typical sentence that a learner might use when you enquire about their weekend or a party.

Example: I went to the beach.

Ask: 'What could you add to the sentence to make it interesting?'

Example: It was so hot on Saturday that I went to the beach to swim in the cool, blue sea.

1 Learners must choose which word in each sentence is more interesting.

Write the example sentence on the board: '"Hold on Tom!" said Alex.' Ask: 'Which word could be changed in the sentence that will show how Alex was talking to Tom?' The learners should identify 'said' and change it to 'shouted'. Ask: 'Which word is more interesting: "said" or "shouted"?' Discuss why 'shouted' is a more interesting word. The response should be that it tells us how Alex spoke to Tom. It also lets us know that Alex was far away. He was at the top of the cliff.

2 Learners work in pairs to make the sentences on page 7 more interesting. They must change the underlined word in each sentence and read the sentence out aloud. Draw the learners' attention to the words in the box: 'waved', 'grinned', 'terrible', 'called'.

Answers
a waved
b grinned
c called
d terrible

When this activity is completed, it would be a good time to introduce synonyms to the learners.

Explain that a synonym is a word that has the same or similar meaning to another word. Use the words from the above activity to illustrate synonyms. Write the underlined words from the above activity on the board and ask learners to give you a word that has a similar meaning: 'moved' – 'waved'; 'smiled' – 'grinned'; 'said' – 'called'; 'bad' – 'terrible'.

Workbook page 3

Vocabulary
The learners must find a word with a similar meaning and write it on the line. Read through the words in the box on the Workbook page with the class.

Answers
a large
b difficult
c start
d tremble
e below
f scream

Weekly review
Use this rubric to assess learners' progress as they worked through the activities this week.

Level	Reading	Writing	Listening and speaking
■	This group can find most regular verbs by reading a section of text. They need support when having to substitute words with similar meanings.	This group needs some support when writing verbs in the correct form.	This group needs some support regarding the correct form of verbs when retelling a story. They need some support to use interesting words.
●	This group can find all regular verbs by reading a section of text. They can substitute many words with words that have similar meanings.	This group can write most verbs using the correct form.	This group is mostly able to use the correct form of verbs when retelling a story. They use some interesting words.
▲	This group can find all regular and most irregular verbs by reading a section of text. They can substitute most words with words that have similar meanings.	This group can write all verbs using the correct form.	This group can retell a story speaking clearly, audibly and uses the correct form of verbs and interesting words.

Week 3
Student's Book pages 7–10

Workbook pages 3–5

Student's Book page 7
Writing
1 Start the lesson by asking:
- Do you remember Tom's friend?
- What kind of friend do you think Alex was?
- Why do you say this?

It may be necessary to do a quick recap of the story if the learners are struggling to come up with the answers. Invite them to imagine that they are Alex and they need to tell a friend what happened to Tom. Have the following words written on cards: 'Where?' 'When?' 'What?' Show them to the class as you ask each of the following questions:

Ask: 'Where did the action happen?' (The action happened at the top of a cliff.) 'When did this happen?' (It happened when Tom looked over the edge of the cliff. It happened when Tom was walking with his friend.) 'What did the place look like?' (It was very high and sheer rock.)

Write the following sentence on the board: 'Yesterday Tom and I went for a walk. We walked …'

Ask the learners to continue with the sentence. Display the cards: 'Where?' 'When?' 'What?' Learners start writing and complete this activity.

Support: Have the beginnings of sentences on cards that the learners could use to help with their sentences.

Student's Book page 8
Writing
2 Before the lesson, gather some books that the learners have read as a class (ask the previous year's teacher for some titles) or collect other well-known stories. Show the books to the learners and ask a few general questions such as:

- What is the story about?
- Where does it take place?
- Who are the characters in the story?
- Did you enjoy the story?

Workbook page 3
Story sequencing
Read through the sentences with the whole class. Ask whether the sentences are in the correct order as it happened in the story. Explain that it is important to put things in the correct order. Learners work alone to complete the activity.

Answers
1 Tom and Alex were walking along the cliff.
2 Tom slipped and fell.
3 Tom held on to the side of the cliff.
4 Alex phoned to get help.
5 A helicopter rescued Tom.

Explain to the learners that when a book is discussed it is called a 'review'. The discussion that they have just done was about the story *The Rescue*. It is important to get the order, or sequence, of events correct when reviewing a story. Say that today they are going to review *The Rescue*.

Student's Book page 8
Writing
2 Discuss the questions with the learners. Remind the learners that it is very important to write the title of the book and the author.

Answers
a The main characters are Tom and Alex.
b The story takes place on a sunny day when Alex and Tom were walking on the cliff top.
c Tom looked over the edge of the cliff when his foot slipped. He slid down the rock face but managed to grab hold of a narrow ledge. Alex went for help. Tom heard a loud noise. A man in a harness came to rescue him. Tom was pulled up to the helicopter.
d Learners' own answers.

3 Hand out PCM 2 to each learner. They start to write a book review about *The Rescue*.

Student's Book page 8
Grammar: Speech marks
Start the discussion by asking learners how they know when someone is speaking in a story. They should be able to identify speech marks. If they are not able to do this, let everyone open their books to *The Rescue*. Read the first paragraph to the learners and ask questions that would lead them to discover the speech marks.

For example: What did Alex shout to Tom? ("Hold on, Tom!") Explain that these were the actual words that Alex said. We know this because of the speech marks. Ask: 'What else did Alex say?' ("Help is on the way!")

Write "Hold on, Tom!" and "Help is on the way!" on the board. Point to the inverted commas and explain to the learners that they tell the reader that those are the actual words that someone is saying in a story. Say that when they see this in a story, it means that the person is talking to someone. This is called a 'dialogue'.

Ask learners to open the Student's Book on page 8. Read the explanation to the learners.

1 Ask the questions. If a learner is unable to answer, point to the board where you wrote the sentences.

Answers
a Alex
b Tom
c He shouted.

2 The learners look for another dialogue in *The Rescue*. Give the learners sufficient time to work through this section. Hold a class discussion on what the learners have found.

Write some sentences on the board and invite a learner to come forward to fill in the speech marks.

Example sentences:

I will come and help you said Ajay ("I will come and help you", said Ajay.)

Please stop that now shouted Jack ("Please stop that now!" shouted Jack.)

Give each learner a copy of PCM 3. Learners fill in the speech marks and other punctuation. They also need to write two speech bubbles.

Student's Book page 9

Reading

1 Read the definition of a jet ski. The learners find a jet ski in the pictures.

2 Learners work in pairs and read the newspaper article *A busy day for firefighters*. Remind learners about breaking up difficult words into syllables. Circulate and listen to them reading.

Learners continue with the questions. When they have finished working through the questions, collect the learner's answers as a class discussion.

Answers
a The first fire was on a small boat at sea.
b There were four fishermen in the boat.
c The firefighters used jet skis.
d They used jet skis because the boat was in shallow water.
e The second fire was in a building in town.
f The firefighters used a fire engine.
g They stopped the fire using powerful jets of water from hosepipes.

Workbook page 4

Reading comprehension

Read through the beginnings and endings of the sentences with the learners. Choose an ending for each sentence and copy it next to the beginning of the sentence.

Answers
a Firefighters work in teams to put out fires.
b Firefighters use jet skis to reach fires on small boats.
c Firefighters use ladders to reach the top of buildings.
d Firefighters use hosepipes to pour water on fires.

Writing

Start this activity by asking learners to look at the pictures of the fire and the jet ski.

Ask: 'What information would you need to give over the telephone to a firefighter?' Continue with the discussion and prompt the learners to give some ideas of how the firefighters would get to the ship and what equipment they might use. Show some images of firefighting equipment to help the discussion. Ask two learners to do some role playing to assist with this activity.

Difficult words should be written on the board for the learners who should add these to their dictionaries.

Ask learners to open their Workbooks at page 4.

1 Read the rubric in the Workbook to the learners. Start the discussion as suggested in the Workbook: 'Yesterday we got a call from a ship in the harbour. There was a fire on the ship. Some fishermen were …'

Discuss what comes next. Suggest some other ways in which they could start the story.

For example:
- On Saturday I was walking along the cliff top when I noticed smoke coming from a ship at sea …
- My dad came running into the house and shouted to my mom for the fire department's telephone number. He had seen …

The learners complete the activity.

Extension: Some learners could add some dialogue into their writing.

Student's Book page 10

Listening and speaking

1 Divide the learners into pairs. Tell the learners to listen very carefully. They must imagine that there is a fire in the school. This is very dangerous. Say that you are going to give them some instructions to remember. They may not talk until you have finished speaking.

These are the instructions:
- Stand up quietly.
- Pick up your school bag.
- Form a line at the door.
- When I open the door, walk quickly and quietly to the playground.
- Sit down and wait for me to call your names.

The learners work in pairs and repeat the instructions to their partner. Check who has remembered all of the instructions. If the response is poor, repeat the instructions and the learners redo the exercise.

2 Invite the learners to give their opinion about the instructions by asking:
- Why did you have to walk quietly?
- Why did you have to wait at the door?

3 Divide the learners into groups. They need to imagine that there is a flood near their house or school. Ask: 'What instructions will you give to your family and friends to keep them out of danger?'

Learners discuss what instructions should be given to keep their family and friends out of danger. Each group should be given an opportunity to report back with their instructions.

Workbook page 5
Grammar and punctuation
Learners read the dialogue together. Draw their attention to the speech marks.

Ask:' What did Mariam ask?' ("Where is the fire?") 'What word tells us how the teacher replied?' (shouted).

Read through the questions with the learners.

Answers
a Mariam
b the teacher
c dangerous
d children, playground
e Learner's own answers, but could include 'shouted', 'yelled', 'screamed', 'bellowed'.

Weekly review
Use this rubric to assess learners' progress as they worked through the activities this week.

Level	Reading	Writing	Listening and speaking
■	This group needs support to sequence events in a story.	This group relies on the structure of a familiar story to develop their own writing with support.	This group requires support to express a logical sequence of events.
●	This group can sequence events in a story.	This group is becoming more successful at using the structure of a familiar story to develop their own writing.	This group talks about and plans their stories well with minimal teacher support.
▲	This group can confidently sequence events in a story.	This group can use the structure of a familiar story to develop their own writing.	This group plans their stories well through discussion.

Unit 2 In the post

Unit overview

The focus for the first and second week is on written communication, looking specifically at the different types of correspondence used for different purposes such as postcards, emails, letters to friends and formal letters. Learners will have the opportunity to research places of interest using the internet. Attention will be given to the appropriate forms of greetings, endings and also the format of different types of letters. Focus on language used for formal and informal letters will be discussed. Also, during the second week, they will look at pronouns. The third week revisits verbs. Learners work with a dictionary and come to understand alphabetical order. The use of the apostrophe is introduced as well as homonyms. Letter writing is extended with the use of paragraphs.

Reading	Writing	Listening and speaking
3R09 Use IT sources to locate simple information;	3W07 Write simple sentences, dictated by the teacher, from memory;	3SL1 Speak clearly and confidently in a range of contexts, including longer speaking turns;
3Rv1 Identify the main purpose of a text;	3W10 Make a record of information drawn from a text, e.g. by completing a chart;	3SL3 Take turns in discussion, building on what others have said;
3Rx1 Answer questions with some reference to single points in a text;	3W09 Use a dictionary or electronic means to find the spelling and meaning of words;	3SL4 Listen and respond appropriately to others' views and opinions.
3Rx3 Identify the main points or gist of a text;	3Wp5 Recognise the use of the apostrophe to mark omission in shortened words, e.g. 'can't', 'don't';	
3Rw3 Consider ways that information is set out on a page and on a screen, e.g. lists, charts, bullet points.	3Wp9 Identify pronouns and understand their function in a sentence;	
	3Wp12 Know irregular forms of common verbs;	
	3Wp13 Ensure grammatical agreement of pronouns and verbs in using standard English;	
	3Wa6 Establish purpose for writing, using features and style based on model texts;	
	3Wa10 Write letters, notes and messages;	
	3Ws2 Explore words that have the same spelling but different meanings (homonyms), e.g. 'form', 'wave';	
	3Ws6 Organise words or information alphabetically using first two letters.	

Related resources:

- Slideshow 2: In the post
- PCM 4: Greetings

Introducing the unit

As this unit is largely about written communication, a fun way to start is to have various types of writing equipment on display, for example: a feather and a bottle of ink, some handmade paper, a fountain pen, sealing wax, a small blackboard and chalk. Make a postbox out of cardboard, with a slot for posting letters in the front and a door at the back to remove the letters. This will be used throughout the unit.

Have some postcards and letters inside the postbox addressed to various learners in your class. Choose a variety of postcards, for example: a picture of an animal, a famous landmark, scenery, a foreign country, art.

Week 1

Student's Book pages 11–12

Ask the learners to look at the items on display. Ask: 'Has anyone ever used any of the items? Have you seen anyone use them? What have they used them for?' The response should be that they were/are used for writing. Draw the learners' attention to the postbox. Ask: 'Where have you seen this? Have you or someone that you know ever used this? What did you use it for?' It may be possible that some of the learners will not know what a postbox is, so explain what it is used for.

Divide the learners into groups. Open the postbox, take out the postcards and read out the names of the learners to whom they are addressed. Give the learners a few minutes to look at the picture and to read the postcard. Start the discussion by asking the learners to describe the picture on the postcard. Ask: 'Would you see this in your country? Can you identify where this is? Why was this postcard sent? What did the postcard tell you?' Talk about how information is set out on a postcard (layout).

Student's Book page 11

Reading and speaking

The learners look at the postcards in the book, discuss and answer the questions.

Answers
a India, China. The pictures on the front and the text tell us this.
b Dickson Amata, Wasima Abdullah
c Mike, Mary
d Learners' own answers.

Student's Book page 12

Listening and speaking

1 Give the learners this assignment before starting this section. Ask them to use the internet to find out some interesting information about the giant pandas in Chengdu and the Taj Mahal in India.

Do some research ahead of time so that you can check the websites in order to give the learners the correct web addresses. Here are some suggestions for giant pandas: www.nationalgeographic.com and www.worldwildlife.org. For the Taj Mahal: www.whc.unesco.org and www.sciencekids.co.nz and there are many more, of course. Draw up list of questions for the learners. Here are some suggestions:

Giant pandas

- How much bamboo does a panda eat every day?
- Find out something interesting about a panda baby.
- Why did the World Wild Life Organisation use the panda as their logo?
- Do you think that the special programmes are protecting the pandas?

Taj Mahal

- How many years did it take to build the Taj Mahal?
- How many people visit the Taj Mahal each year?
- What does 'Taj Mahal' mean?
- In which city will you find the Taj Mahal?
- Is the Taj Mahal well looked after?

2 The learners bring the information to class. Divide the learners into groups and allow them to share their information with each other. Give each group an opportunity to share their information with the rest of the class.

Extension: Learners design their own postcard. They draw a picture of a well-known landmark or building in the area on one side. The postcard will be sent to someone in the class. Use the school address on the postcard. The learners can write something interesting about the landmark or building and post it in the postbox.

The postcards are distributed the next day. Allow learners to comment on the postcard that they have received. How did they feel when they received the postcard? Have they learnt something new?

Weekly review

Use this rubric to assess learners' progress as they worked through the activities this week.

Level	Reading	Listening and speaking
■	This group needs support to read and make sense of postcards and letters.	With support and structure this group can find information and tell others about what they found out.
●	This group is able to work independently to read and make sense of postcards and letters, but they may not always make links between the sources.	This group is able to find relevant information and can summarise what they find to do a presentation.
▲	This group reads confidently and makes sense of the context and content in a range of written sources.	This group is able to work independently to do their own research and can summarise the information and do an interesting and confident presentation.

Week 2

Student's Book pages 12–15

Workbook pages 6–7

Student's Book pages 12–14

Reading and speaking

1 Ask the learners whether they receive letters, postcards or emails from friends or family. Ask: 'When do you receive letters, emails, postcards? Why do people send letters, emails or postcards?'

Answers
For example:
When?
- letters: when someone far away or who lives in a different country wants to tell you a lot of news; when you have won a competition; an invitation to a party or a wedding
- emails: when someone wants to tell you their news; to send you a short message; someone is wanting to sell you something; making a complaint
- postcards: when a friend is visiting a new place or on holiday; to write a short message

Why?
- letters: tell news, ask for information, a complaint, an invitation
- emails: tell news, ask for information, an invitation, an advertisement
- postcards: to write a short message

Have the heading 'In the post' in large letters to pin up on the display board. Below this heading have the words: 'letters', 'emails', 'postcards'. Write the following questions on cards or on a large sheet of paper and pin this up on classroom display board under the three subheadings ('letters', 'emails', 'postcards').

- What sort of text is this?
- Who wrote the text and to whom?
- Why was the text written?

Refer to the above questions while explaining to the learners that this week they are going to look at different types of letters. They are going to find out why letters are written and to whom letters are written. They are also going to look at the language used in letters, whether the language is formal or informal. They are also going to look at how information is set out.

2 Read the notepad feature on Student's Book page 15 about formal and informal language. Give the learners some examples of formal language and informal language.

Example: What words do you use when you greet your teacher or principal? ('Good morning, Mrs/Mr ...' or 'Good morning Ma'am/Sir ...') What words do you use when you greet your friends? (Hi ...)

Letter 1

Ask a learner to read this letter to the class.

The learners work in pairs and answer the questions which appear on the classroom display board, for example:

- What sort of text is this?
- Who wrote the text and to whom?
- Why was the text written?

Encourage the learners to talk about the words used in the letter that have influenced their answers. Discuss the final sentence: 'C U soon!' What does it mean? Why has it been written this way?

Letter 2 and Letter 3

Read through both letters. The learners read the letters out aloud together.

Ask questions such as:

- What sort of texts are these two letters? (Letter 2 is a formal letter and Letter 3 is an informal letter.)
- Why is Letter 2 formal? (The greeting is formal: 'Dear Sir/Madam', and so is the ending: 'Yours faithfully', and the person has written their name and surname.) Explain why 'Yours faithfully' appears at the end of the formal letter. This ending is used when you do not know the person to whom you are writing.
- Why is Letter 3 informal? (An informal letter is about congratulations, an invitation, apologies, or to thank someone. The greeting is just 'Jo' not Miss/Mrs/Mr and there is no surname and the ending is just 'Love'. The word 'Love' implies that this person has a close relationship with the person to whom they are writing.)
- When you look at the layout of the two letters, what do you notice? (Letter 2 has a full address and the date, while Letter 3 has a shortened address and no date.)

Say: Now let's look at the reasons for each text/letter. Give the learners time to read through the letters again.

Ask:

- Why was Letter 2 written? (The letter is a complaint about a product, in this case a game console. Keith Pratt is unhappy with the quality of the product. It is also a request for the item to be replaced.)
- What is the purpose of Letter 3? (It is to wish Jo a happy birthday.)

Letter 4

Ask:

- What is the first difference that you notice about this letter? (It has two addresses.)

Read the addresses to the learners and the letter.

- How do you know which address belongs to the writer, Charlie Gaw? (The address on the right because the other one starts with 'Tolby Toys'.)

Explain to the learners that when you write a formal letter to a business, you write your address and the business' address on the letter. Your address always appears on the right and the business' address on the left.

Ask:

- Why is the letter not addressed to a specific person? (We don't know who will be receiving the letter.)

Ask the questions that appear on the display board:

- What sort of text is this?
- Who wrote the text and to whom?
- Why was the text written?

Letter 5

Learners follow the text in the email while you read aloud. Read the email, including the heading and subject. The learners read the email aloud together.

Draw their attention to the notepad feature at the top of page 15. Ask:

- Who wrote the text and to whom was it written? (Mariam wrote to Maggie.)
- Why was this text written? (It was written to tell a friend about her holiday.)
- What sort of text is this? (It is an informal text.)
- Why do you say this text is informal? (The word 'Hi' is used at the beginning of the letter and 'See you soon!' at the end of the letter.)

Focus the learners' attention on the capital letters in the text. Ask:

- What does it mean when someone uses capital letters in a text? (It means that the person is shouting or they want to emphasise something. Here, Mariam is emphasising the height of the building. You would not find this in a formal text.)

- Look at the punctuation marks in the text. Which punctuation mark, besides a full stop, has been used in the text? (An exclamation mark.) Explain that this also makes the text informal as an exclamation mark is usually used when there is a dialogue. Remind the learners about the dialogue which was covered in Unit 1.

Give the learners PCM 4 and ask them to complete the questions.

Workbook pages 6–7

Reading and understanding

The learners read the letter and answer the questions.

Answers
1 Sanjay wrote this letter.
2 It is to request a catalogue.
3 The offices are in Maharashtra.
4 It is a formal letter. It has two full addresses; the greeting is formal 'Dear Sir/Madam'; the language used is polite; there are no abbreviations or capital letters or exclamation marks; the words at the end are formal, 'Yours faithfully'.
5 The catalogue will be sent to the address on the right-hand side.
6 Sanjay expects to receive a free gift.

Student's Book pages 14–15

Speaking and writing

1 Explain to the learners that they are going to discuss the differences and similarities of the letters. Assist the learners by giving them the page number where the letter appears.

Answers
a Mariam wants to share her holiday experiences with her friend, Maggie.
b Mariam and Maggie are friends. Jo is a child and Aunty Karen is an adult. They are related.
c Mariam's letter begins with 'Hi' and ends with 'See you soon'. Jo's letter to Lee begins with 'Hi' and ends with 'C U soon'.
d It is a formal letter and he does not know who will be receiving the letter.
e A letter and an email can both be formal and informal. An email's address is different to a letter's address. The email address does not always have the person's name – you can use a nickname. An email address does not have the name of the street or town.
f Two addresses are used as it is a formal letter. Also, he wants to receive a free gift and they need to know where to send it to.
g If you know the person to whom you are writing, you might end the letter informally with the word 'love' or 'see you soon' as this indicates that this is a friend. In a formal letter you may not know the person. It would be strange to end a letter with 'love' when you are asking for a catalogue so 'Yours faithfully' is used.

2 Instruct the learners to work in pairs. Tell them to look at the different letters again, then draw and write the information on a chart in their exercise book to show the differences between the types of letters.

Weekly review

Use this rubric to assess learners' progress as they worked through the activities this week.

Level	Reading	Writing
■	This group reads at a slow pace, but still needs some support to interpret the punctuation and the mood of the text.	This group needs support to write a thank you note with correct spelling and appropriate language.
●	This group is reading with increased accuracy and is starting to interpret the punctuation and mood of the text.	This group can write a thank you note in a casual tone. They spell correctly and are beginning to use the past and present tenses of verbs with some accuracy.
▲	This group reads accurately and at a steady pace, correctly interpreting the punctuation and mood of the text.	This group can write a thank you note correctly, using capital letters and full stops and apostrophes. They use the past and present tense of verbs competently.

Week 3

Student's Book pages 15–19

Workbook pages 7–11

Student's Book page 15

Grammar: pronouns and verbs

Spend a few minutes revising nouns with the learners. Explain that pronouns are words that we use in place of nouns in sentences.

Learners open their books and read the teaching text together. Read and discuss the singular and plural form of pronouns.

On the display board, where the adjectives were put up in Unit 1, add the heading 'Pronouns'. Below that have two subheadings: 'Singular' and 'Plural'. Copy the pronouns from the Student's Book onto cards. Distribute them amongst the learners and ask them to put the pronouns under the correct headings.

Look at the sentences. The words in green are pronouns. Read through the sentences together. This is what the sentences would sound like if pronouns were not used: 'Maggie and Maggie's family went to the Burj Kalifa. Maggie's family went up in the lift. The lift was very fast. Maggie enjoyed Maggie's self.'

Ask: 'How do the pronouns change the sentences?' (The pronouns make the sentences easier to read.) 'Why is the pronoun "her" used?' ('Her' is used because it refers to Maggie, who is a girl. In the next sentence 'they' is used instead of family. 'It' refers to the lift.)

1 Learners copy the sentences into their exercise book. They underline the pronouns.

Answers
a <u>We</u> are on holiday in Dubai. <u>It</u> is very hot here.
b <u>I</u> would love <u>you</u> to come.
c <u>He</u> has to switch <u>it</u> off and start again.
d <u>We</u> went up in a lift. <u>It</u> took <u>us</u> up to the observation deck.
e Look forward to seeing <u>you</u> again at the end of the year.

Workbook page 7

Grammar: pronouns

Learners underline the pronouns in the sentences. They tick S for singular and P for plural.

Answers
a <u>They</u> are on holiday in Buenos Aires. P
b He has many aunts and uncles. S
c This is Aunty Nadia. She fetches me from school every day. S
d The lift took <u>us</u> up to the observation deck. P
e The family visits Jamaica every year. <u>We</u> stay with <u>our</u> cousins in Kingston. P

Student's Book page 16

Grammar: pronouns and verbs

2 Spend a few minutes revising verbs. Refer to the 'Verbs' display board that was used in Unit 1. Read through the verbs again, remind learners that verbs are action words, and revise irregular verbs. Learners do the activity, choosing the correct verb for each sentence. They write the correct sentences in their exercise book.

Answers
a visits
b am going
c has
d are having
e was

Read the notepad information. Pronouns must agree with the verbs. Read through the examples. Here are some more:

I **am** going to the party.

We **are going** to the party.

Student's Book page 16

Spelling and vocabulary

Ask the learners to recite the letters of the alphabet. To find words quickly they need to know this order. Learners write the letters in alphabetical order in their exercise book.

Answers
a B C D F G
b A E I O U
c L N O P Q
d S T V W Y

Workbook page 8

Dictionary work

1 Ask the learners to write the letters in alphabetical order.

2 Explain to the learners that they will use the order of the alphabet to put the list of names in alphabetical order.

3 Learners write seven names beginning with *Be* in alphabetical order. They need to use the third letters in each name to do this.

Answers
1 A, B, C, E, G, K, M, P, S
2 Aliya, Gareth, Jenna, Mary, Nicola, Pedro, Sanjay, Wahid
3 The order is: Beatriz, Becky, Begum, Behati, Benjiro, Bernard, Beth.

Student's Book page 17

Grammar: apostrophes

Read the explanation of the apostrophe to the learners. Have some words with apostrophes written on cards. Discuss the words with the learners. Put the cards on the display board below the heading 'Apostrophe'.

1–2 The learners work in pairs. They look at the informal letters and find five sentences with apostrophes. They copy the sentences into their exercise book and circle the words with apostrophes.

Answers
For example: Letter 5
Hope you're enjoying your holiday and that you are well?
As you know, I'm with my family in Dubai for a few days.
It's the tallest building in the world.
But it wasn't.
I didn't want to go down again.
That's all for now.

3 Learners discuss what the complete words are.

Workbook page 9

Grammar: apostrophes

1 The learners rewrite the words using apostrophes.

2 The learners write the words without the apostrophes.

Answers
1 you're, don't, I'm, we'll, it's, haven't
2 I will, let us, we are, they will, can not, would have

3 Learners use some of the words with apostrophes to complete the speech bubbles in the pictures. Give the learners an opportunity to read aloud what they have written in the speech bubbles.

Student's Book page 17

Grammar: apostrophes

4 Start this activity by revisiting verbs on the display board from Unit 1. Remind the learners that verbs are action words. Look at irregular verbs that were covered in Unit 1, such as: 'was terrified', 'are dangerous' etc.

Some verbs change when they describe actions in the past. Read the examples in the Student's Book. Work in pairs. Read the letters again and find the same verbs in different forms.

Answers
is – was
go – went
have – had
think – thought
buy – bought
take – took
do – did

Workbook page 10

Grammar: verbs

1 Learners match verbs in the present tense with their forms in the past tense.

Answers
have – had; is – was; draw – drew; do – did; eat – ate; get – got; go – went; win – won; wake – woke

2 Learners choose three past tense verbs and write a sentence using each verb.

Student's Book pages 17–18

Writing

Explain to the learners that a paragraph is a section of a text. Each paragraph in a letter gives different information. We arrange text in paragraphs so that it is easy to read and understand.

1 Learners write a short message to a friend to invite them to come to their house or on an outing. Post the letter in the postbox. Redistribute the letters to the learners to read to themselves.

2 Learners look at the letters from Aunty Karen and Keith Pratt and then answer the questions.

Answers
a Keith Pratt's letter has two paragraphs. Aunty Karen's letter has three paragraphs.
b Keith Pratt's letter: in the first paragraph the fault is discussed, in the second paragraph a solution to the problem is given. Aunty Karen's letter: in the first paragraph she wishes Jo happy birthday, in the second paragraph she comments on her tests and in the third paragraph she says that she will see her at the end of the year.

3 Ask the learners to look at the letter layout on page 18. Explain that they are going to write a letter to someone in their family about an outing they went on. As you go through the layout ask the learners for suggestions for the different paragraphs.

Workbook page 10

Writing

1–3 Ask the learners to look at the letter. Ask: 'Does this look like a letter? What is wrong with this?' Tell them that they are going to mark all the mistakes on the letter and then rewrite it correctly in their exercise book.

Student's Book pages 18–19

Spelling

Explain that homonyms are words that have the same spelling but different meanings. Ask the learners to read the sentences aloud together. Ask: 'Do the underlined words sound the same? Do they have the same meaning?'

Encourage the learners to use a dictionary if they are unsure of the meanings of the words.

Workbook page 11

Spelling: homonyms

Read the rubric and explanation with the learners. Then ask them to write the definitions.

Answers
1 close: to shut; nearby
2 fair: an event; equal
3 bow: ribbon tied in a certain way; bend at the waist, curtsey
4 left: go away from a place, gone; direction (opposite of right)
5 wind: roll up something, wrap around; breeze, current of air

Weekly review

Use this rubric to assess learners' progress as they worked through the activities this week.

Level	Reading	Writing	Listening and speaking
■	This group reads at a slow pace, but still needs some support to interpret the punctuation and the mood of the text.	This group needs support to write in paragraphs. They can use capital letters and full stops, but need reminding about apostrophes and the correct tenses of verbs.	This group struggles to convey knowledge or facts obtained through research and texts.
●	This group is reading with increased accuracy and is starting to interpret the punctuation and mood of the text.	This group can write in paragraphs using capital letters and full stops and apostrophes. They are beginning to use the past and present tenses of verbs with some accuracy.	This group is able to convey some knowledge or facts obtained through research and texts.
▲	This group reads accurately and at a steady pace, correctly interpreting the punctuation and mood of the text.	This group can write in paragraphs, giving different information in each paragraph, using capital letters and full stops and apostrophes. They use the past and present tense of verbs competently.	This group eagerly conveys knowledge or facts obtained through research and texts. They show a good level of understanding of the topic.

Unit 3 Bugs

Unit overview

In the first week the learners will read an extended poem and answer questions. They will be made aware of looking at punctuation marks and rhyming words when reciting a poem. They will be given an opportunity to write their own poem. In the second and third week, focus is on non-fiction texts about a different type of bug, namely germs. Compound words are introduced and nouns, verbs, adjectives and synonyms are revisited. At the end of week three, there is a formal assessment which will cover the work of Units 1, 2 and 3.

Reading	Writing	Listening and speaking
3R01 Use effective strategies to tackle blending unfamiliar words to read, including sounding out, separating into syllables, using analogy, identifying known suffixes and prefixes, using context; 3Rv1 Identifying the main purpose of a text; 3Rv2 Understand and use the terms 'fact', 'fiction' and 'non-fiction'; 3Rx1 Answer questions with some reference to single points in text; 3Rx3 Identify the main points or gist of a text; 3R04 Practise learning and reciting poems; 3R05 Read aloud with expression to engage the listener; 3R07 Use knowledge of punctuation and grammar to read age-appropriate texts with fluency, understanding and expression.	3W05 Identify misspelt words in own writing and keep individual spelling logs; 3W07 Write simple sentences, dictated by the teacher, from memory; 3W09 Use a dictionary or electronic means to find the spelling and meaning of words; 3W10 Make a record of information drawn from a text, e.g. by completing a chart; 3Wp8 Collect examples of nouns, verbs, adjectives, and use the terms appropriately; 3Wa5 Generate synonyms for high frequency words, e.g. 'big', 'little', 'good'; 3Wa9 Write and perform poems, attending to the sound of words; 3Wp1 Maintain accurate use of capital letters and full stops in showing sentences and check by reading own writing aloud; 3Ws1 Use effective strategies to tackle segmenting unfamiliar words to spell, including segmenting into individual sounds, separating into syllables, using analogy, identifying known suffixes and prefixes, applying known spelling rules, visual memory, mnemonics; 3Ws5 Use and spell compound words.	3SL3 Take turns in discussion, building on what others have said; 3SL4 Listen and respond appropriately to others' views and opinions; 3SL5 Listen and remember a sequence of instructions.

Related resources

- Audio files: *Bugs!*; How to wash your hands; Flies
- Slideshow 3: Bugs
- PCM 5: Finding facts about germs
- PCM 6: Matching pairs
- PCM 7: Hand washing poster

Introducing the unit

Ask the learners to design and build, or draw, a small creature that has never been seen before. Encourage them to use recyclable materials such as egg cartons, cans, plastic containers and so on. The learners bring them to class. Create a display, with some suspended from the ceiling and others climbing the wall. Give the learners an opportunity to discuss their constructions. Find out from the learners if they were influenced by a particular creature that already exists. At the end of the discussion ask the learners if there is something similar in their constructions such as number of legs, and talk about whether their creatures have wings, antennae, eyes, etc. Ask learners what word could be used to describe their creatures. The learners may suggest 'insects', but this should be discarded as insects have particular characteristics. If necessary, suggest the word 'bugs' as this covers a wide range of creatures with some similar characteristics.

Week 1

Student's Book pages 20–23

Workbook page 12

Student's Book pages 20–21

Reading and speaking

1 Ask the learners to complete the definition of the word 'bug', for example: 'A bug is a small insect. It is also something that causes a fault in a computer, or a germ.'

2 Divide the poem *Bugs* into sections. Allocate the sections to a corresponding number of learners who read the poem aloud to the class. Afterwards, ask the whole class to read the poem together. Ask them whether they enjoyed the poem. Did they find it funny? Did they learn something new?

Student's Book page 22

Reading and speaking

1 Discuss and answer the questions about the poem

Answers
a Bugs can upset your tummy and make your nose runny. They can turn good food bad, and they make things smell.
b Bugs make things rot and make food for trees.
c You will find bugs in the water, in the air, everywhere.
d Bugs help reduce rubbish that gets thrown away. They cause old leaves to rot and decay which is food for trees and plants.
e Cuts must be covered with a plaster to keep the bugs away.
f Yes, bugs can make you ill because they turn food bad.

Workbook page 12

Reading and understanding

Answers
1 false; **b** false; **c** true; **d** false; **e** true; **f** true; **g** true; **h** false

Student's Book page 22

2 Read the tips for reading aloud and reciting a poem. Discuss what it means to read with expression. Illustrate to the learners how to read with expression. Divide the learners into groups. The learners read the poem aloud with expression in their groups.

Read the notepad feature about exclamation marks. Ask the learners to look for exclamation marks in the poem. They read the poem again.

Workbook page 12

Reading aloud and phonics

Learners read the words aloud. They fill in the blanks with the rhyming words from the box.

Answers
a wear; **b** me; **c** should; **d** ill; **e** away; **f** grow; **g** do; **h** funny; **i** trees; **j** bad

Student's Book pages 22–23

Listening and speaking

Before starting this discussion, show the learners the international symbol for recycling. Ask if they know what this signs means. Where have they seen this? Show some items that have this sign to the learners, for example: a plastic carrier bag, a bottle, a cardboard box and so on. Ask the learners to explain ways in which the items can be recycled and reused.

Discuss the questions in the Student's Book with the learners.

- What do you do with leaves and vegetable peels at home?
- Can you reuse these in any way?
- Do you have a compost heap?
- What is the best thing to do with leaves and vegetable peelings? Why?

Writing

1 Revise the definition of nouns, verbs and adjectives. Explain to the learners that they are going to find examples of these in the poem *Bugs*. They are going to write the examples in their exercise book under the headings 'nouns', 'verbs', 'adjectives'.

Answers

nouns	verbs	adjectives
bugs	talk	good
poem	wrote	small
creatures	see	very
indoors	in	funny
outdoors	look	runny
everywhere	(are)on	much
hands	(are) in	good
hair	make	more
clothes	get	such
tummy	heal	rot
nose	take	smell

plaster	turning	decay
pill	cause	
food	tell	
pile	owe	
stuff	need	
friends	grow	
mountains		
soil		
year		
leaves		
apple		
potato		
skin		
core		

2 Explain to the learners that they are going to write their own poem. They can use some of the nouns, verbs and adjectives that they have written down. Remind the learners about the rhyming words from the poem *Bugs*:

Hair	wear
decay	away
runny	funny
you	do
mad	bad

The learners use the writing frame to start their poem.

Weekly review

Use this rubric to assess learners' progress as they worked through the activities this week.

Level	Reading	Writing
■	This group need lots of support and prompting to learn and recite the poem.	These learners compile a short list of known words and stick to the familiar words from the text to develop their own poems.
●	This group can learn and recite a poem, but they are not fully confident in their performance.	These learners are able to compile a comprehensive list and add to these to complete their own poems.
▲	This group is able to learn and recite the poem without support and they do a confident and entertaining recitation.	These learners compile a comprehensive list but use creative alternatives to develop their own poems.

Week 2

Student's Book pages 23–26

Workbook pages 13–14

Student's Book page 23

Spelling: compound words

Write a few compound words on cards, for example: 'everyone', 'bedroom', 'playground', 'sunscreen', 'lampshade'.

Ask learners to read the words aloud. Ask: 'Can you find short words in these words?' As the learners identify the short words, cut up the compound words so they can see the two short words.

> everyone – every one
>
> bedroom – bed room
>
> playground – play ground
>
> sunscreen – sun screen
>
> lampshade – lamp shade

Remind the learners that a compound word is made up of two shorter words. Take two of the short words from above and put them together, for example, 'play' + 'room'. Ask the learners to read the word, separate them again and then read the two short words.

Workbook page 13

Spelling and grammar

The learners find eight compound words in the word snake. They circle the words and then divide each the word into two parts.

Answers
some/one; bed/room; post/card; under/ground; card/board; out/side; note/book; tooth/paste

Student's Book page 23

Spelling: compound words

Read the notepad feature.

1 The learners work in pairs and write down the two shorter words that make up the compound word.

2 Explain to the learners that they are going to make six compound words with the shorter words and write them in their exercise book.

Answers
1 underground – under ground; outdoors – out doors; everywhere – every where; something – some thing; notebook – note book; toothbrush – tooth brush

2 bookcase, outside, postcard, cupboard, indoors, bedroom

Student's Book pages 24–26

Reading and speaking

1 Ask the learners to read all the headings and look at the illustrations. The learners work in pairs to discuss the questions.

Answers
a The text is about germs, about different kinds of germs and how to protect yourself against germs.
b The text is factual.

The learners then read the texts below each heading. Remind them to use their dictionaries if there are words that they don't understand.

2 Learners read the text again and say if the statements are true or false.

Answers
a true; **b** false; **c** true; **d** false; **e** true; **f** true

Writing

Ask the learners to identify the different types of germs. Encourage them to turn to pages 24–25 to find the information. Discuss where the germs live and what they do.

Read the rubric to the learners. Explain that a chart can be used to record information.

Types of germs	Where they live	What they do
bacteria	outside and inside our bodies	cause infections, help to digest our food, help to form compost
viruses	inside our bodies	cause diseases like AIDS, flu and chickenpox
fungi	dark, damp places	cause skin rashes
protozoa	wet conditions, water	cause tummy infections

Extension: More able learners can carry out a research project using books and/or the internet to find out more about different kinds of germs. They should find at least six facts about germs and check each one by referring to a different source for verification. Once they've done this, they can prepare a short informative talk about germs and what they have learnt. Hand out PCM 5 to help learners structure and record their findings.

Workbook pages 13–14
Reading and understanding

1 Ask the learners to read the text 'Different kinds of germs' from the text *Germs* again. Match the beginning of each sentence with the correct ending.

2 Learners should work alone to answer the questions. Remind them to use complete sentences.

Answers
1c; 2f; 3g; 4e; 5d; 6a; 7b
2a Germs are minute living organisms. They are so small that you need to use a microscope to see them.
b Bacteria and virus are types of germs. They live inside and outside our bodies. Fungi live in a dark, damp places. Protozoa live in wet conditions.
c Most germs are spread through the air.
d Protect yourself from germs by washing your hands and by covering your mouth when you cough or sneeze.

Weekly review

Use this rubric to assess learners' progress as they worked through the activities this week.

Level	Reading	Writing
■	Learners need support and guidance to read factual information and then find the answers to a few of the easier questions.	Learners need support and guidance to complete a chart summarising what they have learnt.
●	Learners can work in pairs or groups to make sense of factual text and find the answers to most of the questions.	Learners can complete a chart to summarise what they have learnt but they do not include all information and they don't summarise information very well.
▲	Learners are able to work independently to read factual text and can easily and correctly find the answers to questions using the text.	Learners can correctly complete a chart to summarise what they have read, paraphrasing and using short points to do so.

Week 3

Student's Book pages 26–27

Workbook pages 14–16

Workbook page 14
Spelling and grammar

This activity serves as a revision of grammar that has been covered in Units 1, 2, 3. Revise the definitions of 'nouns', 'verbs', 'adjectives' and 'pronouns'. Have these definitions written on cards and pin them onto the display boards.

1 The learners must find three nouns, three verbs, three, adjectives and three pronouns in the text and write it in the table.

Answers

nouns	verbs	adjectives	pronouns
germs	are	minute	our
organisms		different	they

bacteria	live	types	us
infections	can cause		
food	can help		
viruses	make		
bodies			

Student's Book page 26
Vocabulary: synonyms

Start the lesson by talking about adjectives. Ask: 'How do adjectives improve a sentence?' (Adjectives tells us more about the noun, they make a sentence interesting.)

Write these examples on the board:
- The small boy bumped his head.
- We have a big garden.

Read the teaching text. Remind the learners that they have used synonyms before in Unit 1, Danger! Read the synonyms for 'small' and 'big'. Ask the learners to look at the two examples on the board. Ask them to use a synonym for the adjectives.

- The little boy bumped his head.
- We have a huge garden.

The learners read through the sentences together.

Ask the learners to write the new sentences in their exercise books and to underline the synonyms that they have used.

Answers
a minute; **b** tiny; **c** tall; **d** enormous/huge; **e** huge/gigantic/enormous; **f** little/tiny

Support: Place learners in small groups. Hand out PCM 6 to each group. Let them cut out the cards and arrange them in pairs of synonyms. Once they are familiar with the words, they can also use the cards to play a memory game. Shuffle them, arrange them all face down and take turns to turn over two cards. If they are synonyms, the learner can keep them and score a point. If not, they turn them face down again and the next person takes a turn to choose two cards. The aim is to remember the position of the words so that you can find synonyms when you need to.

Workbook page 15
Vocabulary: synonyms
Learners find four synonyms for 'small' and four synonyms for 'big' in the word puzzle.

Answers
'small': minute, tiny, little, baby; 'big': huge, gigantic, enormous, great

Student's Book page 27
Spelling
Ask the learners to work in pairs. They should read the words aloud and work through the three tasks.

You may have to give the learners some clues about words that end with *–tion*.

Examples: communicate – communication; punctuate – punctuation; pollute – pollution; instruct – instruction

Explain that sometimes the suffix *–tion* is written *–sion*, for example, 'comprehension', 'discussion'.

Workbook page 15
Spelling
Ask the learners to read the sentences. There are two spelling mistakes in each sentence. Underline the spelling mistakes and rewrite each sentence correctly.

a Bakteria can cause infeksions.

Bacteria can cause infections.

b Their are bugs everywear in the world.

There are bugs everywhere in the world.

c I drew a pikture of the little bug in my notbook.

I drew a picture of the little bug in my notebook.

d This book has lots of informasion about inseks.

This book has lots of information about insects.

Workbook page 16
Spelling and vocabulary
Learners underline the correct sentence in each pair.

Answers
a Flies can carry germs **b** Flies have sticky hairs on their feet **c** Germs can give you a sore tummy **d** You can't see germs because they are invisible without a microscope

Student's Book page 27
Listening and speaking
1 Ask the learners to listen carefully as you give the following instructions.

How to wash your hands

Washing your hands is very important as it helps to get rid of germs that can make you sick. This is how you should wash your hands.

- Use clean water and soap.
- Wet your hands and rub some soap on them.
- Rub your hands together for about 20 seconds. Make sure you put soap all over your hands – between your fingers and under your nails. Scrub your hands with a small brush if they are very dirty.
- Count slowly from 1 to 20 while you are washing or say two verses from the *Bugs* poem you have learnt.
- Dry your hands on a clean towel or let them dry in the air.

2 Learners work with a partner and take turns to tell each other how to wash their hands properly. Circulate while the learners are giving the instructions.

Extension: Learners work in groups to prepare a poster for younger learners to teach them about the importance of hand washing for health. Hand out PCM 7 for learners to use to make notes to structure and plan their posters. Remind them that young learners may not be able to read well, so they need to make their posters simple, with illustrations to help learners make sense of the information.

Student's Book page 27
Listening and writing
1–2 Tell learners they are going to listen to information about how flies help to spread diseases. Read the information (below) through once or twice as necessary. Then ask the learners to complete the chart. They can work in pairs if they find this difficult.

> One fly can carry nearly two million germs! Flies have tiny pads on their feet which are covered in sticky hairs. These hairs help the fly to stick to anything. They also help germs to stick to the fly.
>
> If a fly lands in a rubbish heap, bits of rubbish and germs stick to the fly's feet. Then when the fly lands on something else, like an apple that you are about to eat, it will bring tiny bits of rubbish and invisible germs with it. These germs will go inside your body when you eat the apple. You may get a sore tummy or diarrhoea.

Workbook page 16
Writing
1 Learners rewrite the paragraph using capital letters, full stops and exclamation marks. Encourage them to read their work aloud to check their punctuation.

Answers
I hate flies! They are noisy because they buzz around all the time. They also sit on your food and on your body. I always chase them away. Uncle James says that they can carry germs too!

2 Tell the learners they are going to write a short story about a fly that spreads germs from a rubbish heap to the food that a family eats. Remind them to use adjectives in their story.

Discuss the instructions with the class. Make sure they understand what each instruction involves. Ask questions to check.

Weekly review
Use this rubric to assess learners' progress as they worked through the activities this week.

Level	Writing	Listening and speaking
■	These learners struggle to plan and write an extended story in paragraphs and use only a limited number of simple sentence constructions.	Learners struggle to listen to instructions and don't remember what to do afterwards.
●	With some support, these learners can plan and write a story in paragraphs and they show some use of a variety of sentence structures, including at least one compound sentence.	Learners listen to instructions and can remember most of them correctly.
▲	Learners are able to plan and write a cohesive story in paragraphs, with a wide variety of sentence types, including compound and complex sentences.	Learners listen attentively to instructions and can remember and follow them accurately.

Formal assessment 1

Use the test on pages 111–114 to assess how well the learners have managed to cover the objectives from the first three units. Hand out the sheets and let the learners complete them under test conditions. Collect and mark their tests, recording the results in your class record book. Take note of any weak areas that you may need to revisit over the next few lessons.

Use the mark scheme below.

Question 1

Reading (7)

A non-fiction (1)

B It means that they could not breathe properly or that they did not have enough oxygen tanks. (2)

C They took photographs, buried a few sweets and a small cross. (any two) (2)

D Queen Elizabeth II was crowned and the news of their ascent reached London. (2)

Question 2

Grammar and vocabulary (23)

A Here are a few possible answers. There are many more. (9)

nouns	verbs	adjectives
climbers	tried	highest
years	led	many
summit	came	climbing

B Rewrite the sentence using speech marks. (2)

"It took the whole team to get us to the summit," answered Edmund Hillary.

(1 mark for set of inverted commas used correctly, 1 mark for comma after 'summit')

C Make four compound words from the words below. (4)

within, photograph, somewhere, somebody, nobody, nowhere

D Read *At the top!* Find synonyms for the following words: (3)

attempted – tried

last – final

yearly – annually

E Write the words in alphabetical order. (1)

cross Edmund oxygen second summit

F Write the words using an apostrophe. (3)

they had – they'd

we will – we'll

were not – weren't

Question 3

Writing (15)

Address (1) note the address will basically be: Top of Mount Everest, 29 May 1953

Greeting (1)

Three separate paragraphs consisting of: opening sentence, content paragraph, ending of letter. (3) Content paragraph should have at least three sentences. (1)

Incorporation of key words and tone of the letter. (2)

Spelling and grammar

- 1–3 spelling and grammar errors (3)
- 4–6 spelling and grammar errors (2)
- 7 or more spelling and grammar errors (1)
- Contents (4)
- Sentences (three or more) must express emotion.
- Sentences must be relevant to the topic.
- Letter must be coherent from the beginning to the end.
- If only one sentence has been written for the content paragraph, 1 mark.

Unit 4 At the library

Unit overview

This unit is about books and different types of stories. In the first week fiction and non-fiction books and texts are discussed. Using the Dewey decimal classification system the learners will find out how books are classified and organised. In the second week the learners will embark on a reading project which will result in a book review and an oral presentation. The learners will read a biography and use the text to answer questions. Simple and compound sentences are discussed and pronouns revisited. During the third week the learners will improve their writing skills specific to their book reviews and practise their letter writing skills. Spelling rules for plurals ending in –y are learnt. The unit ends with a poem.

Reading	Writing	Listening and speaking
3R02 Read a range of story, poetry and information books and begin to make links between them;	3W07 Write simple sentences, dictated by the teacher, from memory;	3SL1 Speak clearly and confidently in a range of context, including longer speaking turns;
3R03 Read and comment on books by the same author;	3W10 Make a record of information drawn from text, e.g. by completing a chart;	3SL3 Take turns in discussion, building on what others have said;
3R05 Read aloud with expression and engage the listener;	3Wa5 Generate synonyms for high frequency words, e.g. 'big', 'little', 'good';	3SL6 Practise to improve performance when reading aloud.
3R06 Sustain the reading of 48–64 page books, noting how a text is organised into sections or chapters;	3Wa8 Write book reviews summarising what a book is about;	
3R09 Use IT sources to locate simple information;	3Wa10 Write letters, notes and messages;	
3R11 Locate books by classification;	3Wp2 Use a wider variety of sentence types including simple, compound and some complex sentences;	
3Ri2 Infer the meaning of unknown words from context;	3Wp4 Vary sentence openings, e.g. with adverbials;	
3Rw1 Consider how choice words can heighten meaning;	3Wp9 Identify pronouns and understand their function in a sentence;	
3Rv1 Identify the main purpose of a text;	3Wp10 Understand that verbs are necessary for meaning in a sentence;	
3Rv2 Understand and use the terms 'fact' and 'non-fiction';	3Wp11 Understand pluralisation and use the terms 'singular' and 'plural';	
3Rv3 Identify different types of stories and typical story themes.	3Wp13 Ensure grammatical agreement of pronouns and verbs in using standard English;	
	3Ws1 Use effective strategies to tackle segmenting unfamiliar words to spell, including segmenting into individual sounds, separating into syllables, using analogy, identifying known suffixes and prefixes, applying known spelling rules, visual memory, mnemonics.	

Related resources:

- Slideshow 4: At the library
- PCM 8: Judging a book by its cover

Introducing the unit

Have some book titles written up on a large poster. Use titles that are familiar to the learners. You could use titles of stories that were covered in the previous stage or even the names of movies that are based on books. Sometimes, bookshops have large promotional posters that they may be happy to let you use. You can also use Slideshow 2 (digital resources) to show a range of book covers.

Go to the school or public library and take out a selection of age-appropriate fiction and non-fiction books for a display in the classroom. Start the lesson by asking the learners to read the poster. What do the words tell them? The response could be either that they are the titles of books or the titles of movies. Ask the learners to try and identify the type of story of each title. You may have to provide some prompts such as: 'Is it an adventure, fantasy, true life story or a folk tale?' Ask the learners if they have read a book that was based on facts, maybe about an important event that happened in their country or about someone who discovered something.

Refer to the books that you selected from the library. Read a few titles. After each title ask the learners to suggest the type of story. Draw their attention to the picture on the cover and ask whether this gives them an idea of the story. Remind them about the non-fiction text they read in Unit 3 about germs. Discuss whether the book titles give a clue as to the texts being fiction or non-fiction.

Week 1

Student's Book pages 28–32

Workbook pages 17–18

Student's Book pages 28–29

Listening and speaking

1 Divide the learners into groups. Give them the three questions:

a What type of books do you enjoy?

b If you enjoy fiction, what type of stories do you enjoy?

c If you enjoy factual books, what subjects do you enjoy?

Ask the learners to open their books at page 28 and to have a look at the suggestions that appear for fiction and non-fiction books.

While the discussions are taking place, circulate and ensure that everyone is participating. After sufficient time, allow each group to report on their findings. While a group is giving some feedback, write on the board the types of books that the group likes. Once all groups have done their report, ask the learners to look at the information that you have put on the board. Ask:

- What type of book is the most popular?
- What type of book is the least popular?
- Is fiction or non-fiction more popular? Why?

At this point inform the learners about the project that they will do in this unit. Say: 'You are soon going to do a project about books written by one author. As you work through these activities, look out for ideas about books that you would like to read.'

2 The learners work in pairs. They open their books at page 28 and look at the names of the books on the list and discuss what type of book each one is. Their opinions may vary, but encourage them to give reasons for their decisions.

3 Ask the learners to look at the list of books again. Ask the questions.

Answers
a the author's name is first; b the family names are first; c yes; d lists are put in alphabetical order to make it easier to find a name, or title, or type; e words in a dictionary, a class list, books in a library, shops in a shopping centre directory

Workbook page 17

Reading and writing

1 The learners read the titles of the books. They then discuss the questions and write the answers.

When the learners have completed this activity, have a discussion about what they have written. Encourage the learners to motivate their answers: Which words in the titles led you to your answers?

2 Ask the learners to make an alphabetical list of the authors of the books. Remind the learners to write the family name (surname) of the author first.

Answers
2 Carpenter, Harry: Mr Majeika

Dahl, Roald: The BFG
Jarman, Julia: Harry the Clever Spider
Laird, Elizabeth: Brown Bear and Wilbur Wolf
Laird, Elizabeth: The Fastest Boy in the World
Russell, Rachel Renee: Oak Diaries

Extension: Use PCM 8 to further explore book covers and to introduce the idea that the cover can make you want to read a book or not. Learners can use any available story books for the activity. Let them share their ideas with a partner or small group once they have completed the activity.

Student's Book pages 29–30
Reading
This lesson is about the Dewey decimal classification system.

1 The learners open their books at page 29 and read *The Dewey decimal system* aloud together.

2 Explain to the learners that they are going to use the Dewey classification list to find information. They must write their answers in their exercise books.

Answers
a 900–999; **b** 500–599; **c** 600–699;
d 900–999; **e** 700–799; **f** 200–299; **g** 700–799

Extension: Display a collection of books from each section of the Dewey decimal system. Ask learners to find and write a book title for each section.

Student's Book pages 30–31
Reading and writing
Remind the learners about a book review. It is a summary of the story with some personal opinions about whether the book was enjoyable or not.

1 Ask the learners to read the two book reviews by themselves, then as a class aloud together.

2 Ask the learners to write their answers to the questions in their exercise books.

Answers
1 They were written to give you an idea of the story and to make you want to read the story.
2 a fiction; **b** adventure, realistic; **c** Uma Krishnaswami; **d** Swapnagiri, India; **e** under *L* for 'Laird' and under *K* for 'Krishnaswami'; **f** find the names of two more books by each author. They find reviews of the books and choose one book that they might like to read.

Workbook page 18
Reading and understanding
1 Ask the learners to read the review of *Oranges in No Man's Land* again. Then they tick the sentences that are correct.

2 Ask the learners to read the review of *The Grand Plan to Fix Everything* again. Then they rewrite the sentences using the correct word.

Answers
1a *Oranges in No Man's Land* is set during the civil war in Lebanon. ✓
b *Oranges in No Man's Land* is set during a civil war in India.
c Ayesha lives with her father and mother in a flat.
d Ayesha's mother becomes ill and she dies. ✓
e Ayesha goes out on the streets in the middle of the war to get medicines for her grandmother. ✓
2 a doesn't; **b** Bombay; **c** adores; **d** funny; **e** writing emails and text messages

Student's Book page 32
Writing
Remind the learners of the chart that they used in *Germs* where they sorted the germs by type, where they lived and what they did. Explain that here they are going to complete a chart for the two books reviewed so far: *Oranges in No Man's Land* and *The Grand Plan to Fix Everything*.

1 The learners copy the chart into their exercise book and complete it.

Answers

Title	Oranges in No Man's Land	The Grand Plan to Fix Everything
Author	Elizabeth Laird	Uma Krishnaswami
Setting	a flat in Lebanon	a tiny town, Swapnagiri, in India
Characters	Ayesha	Dini, Maddie
Type of story	realistic	realistic, comic

2 Explain to the learners that they are going to use this information to write a short note to a friend. Do a quick review on how to write a note. Ask: 'Is it a formal or informal note?' How will you start your note? How will you end your note? How will you make your sentences interesting? Encourage learners to think of adjectives or synonyms that they could use.

Vocabulary

1 Learners work in pairs and work out the meaning of the words used in the book review. Then they use a dictionary to see if they are correct. Draw their attention to the notepad feature which prompts them to read the whole sentence again to try and work out the meaning.

2 Ask the learners to look at the underlined words in the pairs of sentences. Ask: 'Which words do you think will catch the attention of the reader? Why?'

3 Before learners start with the next exercise, revise adjectives using the underlined words from this exercise. The learners use their exercise books to copy the sentences, replacing the underlined words with more interesting words.

Answers

1a civil war: when people (civilians, residents, nationals) of a country fight against each other as opposed to a foreign country fighting against another country
b rocket attack: a rocket shaped weapon which explodes on impact
c idol: someone you or many others admire
d addicted to: a habit, something that you think you can't live without

2 addicted: tells us that she is devoted to watching movies, spends a lot of her time watching movies
gripping: holds your attention, you want to keep on reading
fascinating: captures your interest, you want to read more

3a good: gripping, exciting, excellent
b nice: interesting, fascinating
c likes: enjoys, is addicted to, adores, loves
don't like: dislike, detest, disapprove of
d very big: huge, enormous, massive, gigantic

Project

In preparation for the work the learners will do in weeks 2 and 3, ask them to go to the library and find two or three books by one author. The books should each be 48–64 pages long and have several chapters. This will allow the learners enough time to read the books before they begin their project.

Weekly review

Use this rubric to assess learners' progress as they worked through the activities this week.

Level	Reading	Writing	Listening and speaking
■	This group reads at a slow pace, but still needs some support to interpret the punctuation and the mood of the text.	This group requires support to source the information from texts in order to answer questions.	This group struggles to express their own opinions. They tend to repeat the interpretations of others.
●	This group is reading with more expression and has a fair understanding of correctly interpreting the mood of the text.	This group is mostly able to draw information from texts in order to answer questions.	This group is able to express their opinions, but need support to present them logically.
▲	This group reads with expression and understanding, correctly interpreting the mood of the text.	This group is able to draw information from texts in order to answer questions.	This group expresses their opinions clearly and logically.

Week 2

Student's Book pages 33–37

Workbook pages 19–20

Student's Book pages 33–34

Grammar

1 Explain to the learners that they are going to read some sentences. There is something missing from each sentence. They are going to work in pairs to find out what is missing. When they have completed the exercise, they take turns to read their sentences aloud to the class. Remind the learners that the sentences must be grammatically correct.

Answers
1 There <u>is/was</u> a civil war in the country.
People <u>are/were</u> against each other.
Ayesha's mother <u>was killed</u> in a rocket attack.
Her grandmother <u>was</u> ill.
They <u>were moving</u> to China next month
She <u>was convinced</u> that life in India would be very boring.
I <u>enjoy</u> fantasy stories. They are so predictable and silly!

Ask the learners what was missing from each sentence? (A verb was missing.) Ask them which sentences were the most interesting and why. Draw the learners' attention to the notepad feature about verbs.

Simple and compound sentences

Write this sentence on the board: 'Uma Krishnaswami is an author.' Ask the learners to identify the verb: *is*. Explain that a sentence with one verb is called a 'simple sentence'.

Write the following sentence on the board: 'I like Uma Krishnaswami's books. They are always funny.' Ask the learners to identify the verbs: *like*, *are*. Underline them on the board.

Ask:' Are these two sentences simple sentences? Why?' (Yes, because each sentence has a verb.) What word could be used to join the sentences to make it into a longer sentence? ('because') Add the word 'because' in the sentence and change the relevant punctuation: 'I like Uma Krshnaswami's books because they are always funny.'

Ask the learners to read the sentence aloud. Explain that this sentence which has two verbs is called a 'compound sentence'.

2 Learners open their books at page 33 and read the teaching text aloud. Explain to them that they are going to read the next paragraph aloud and find the verbs in the sentences. When they have finished reading the paragraph, go over the verbs with the learners.

3 Explain to the learners that they are going to draw a table in their exercise books with two headings: 'Simple sentences' and 'Compound sentences'. They are going to copy the sentences into the correct column on the table, underlining the verbs in each sentence.

Answers
1 I <u>have</u> read *Fantastic Mr Fox* and I <u>have</u> seen the film *Charlie and the Chocolate Factory*. Roald Dahl <u>wrote</u> both of these stories. He <u>became</u> a famous writer because he <u>wrote</u> such wonderful stories. Children and adults all over the world <u>have</u> enjoyed his stories. Perhaps his stories <u>are</u> fascinating because he <u>had</u> such an interesting life. He <u>was</u> a boxing champion and he <u>was</u> also a fighter pilot.

2

Simple sentences	Compound sentences
Roald Dahl <u>wrote</u> both of these stories.	I <u>have</u> read *Fantastic Mr Fox* and I <u>have</u> seen the film *Charlie and the Chocolate Factory*.
Children and adults all over the world <u>have</u> enjoyed his stories.	He <u>became</u> a famous writer because he <u>wrote</u> such wonderful stories.
	Perhaps his stories <u>are</u> fascinating because he <u>had</u> such an interesting life.
	He <u>was</u> a boxing champion and he <u>was</u> also a fighter pilot.

Workbook page 19

Grammar

1 The learners complete the sentences using verbs from the box provided. They must be careful as not all the words in the box are verbs.

2 Next, learners must join sentences from the left column to sentences in the right column to make compound sentences and write the compound sentences on the lines.

Answers
1a The Dewey decimal system <u>organises</u> books according to numbers. If you <u>want</u> a book about Africa, you should <u>look</u> at the books with numbers from 900 to 999 in the library.
b "We <u>arrange</u> fiction books in alphabetical order according to the family name of the author," <u>explained</u> the librarian.
2 Some of these books are fiction and some of them are non-fiction.
We were tired so we went home.
They have been to Dubai and they have also been to Bangkok.
I enjoy reading the *Asterix* books because the characters are so funny.
She was bored so she downloaded a book on her tablet.
We can't go to the library today because it is closed.

Student's Book page 34
Reading
Write the word 'biography' on the board. Ask the learners to look up this word in their dictionaries.

Biography: account of a person's life written by another *(Oxford dictionary)*

Write the word 'autobiography' on the board. Ask the learners to look up this word in their dictionaries.

Autobiography: written account of one's own life *(Oxford dictionary)*

In summary, a biography is a text about a person's life written by someone else. An autobiography is a text about a person's life written by that person.

Remind the learners about the project that they are going to do about an author in this week. Tell them that biographies and autobiographies will give them lots of information about why an author writes a certain type of book.

Ask the learners to open their books at page 34. Explain that they are going to read a biography about Elizabeth Laird, the author of the story *Oranges in No Man's Land*.

Ask the learners to read the questions aloud together. They work with a partner and read the biography and answer the questions.

Answers
a Wellington, New Zealand; b India, Ethiopia and Lebanon; c fiction, real-life stories, retellings of folk tales; d boys who ride camels in races in the Middle East; d yes, she is a successful writer because her stories have been published; e living in Lebanon during the civil war

Student's Book page 35
Grammar
Learners read the teaching text and example aloud. In their exercise books they replace the underlined nouns with pronouns.

Answers
1 a she; **b** It; **c** him; **d** He; **e** They; **f** It

Workbook page 20
Grammar
Learners must replace the underlined nouns with pronouns from the box.

Answers
a he; **b** It; **c** They; **d** her; **e** them; **f** She

Student's Book pages 36–37
Reading and speaking
Draw the learners' attention to the information in the notepad about verbs. Ask them to complete the activity, choosing the correct form of the verbs each time.

Answers
a writes; **b** lives; **c** enjoys; **d** have

1–5 Inform the learners that this is the project that you spoke about in the previous week. This is what they are going to do:

- Choose a fiction or non-fiction author.
- Work alone.
- Go to the library and find two or three books by one author. The books should each be 48–64 pages long and have several chapters. (**Note:** the learners will have done this at the end of week 1.)
- Use the internet to find out information for a biography about the author you have chosen.

- Write a short biography about the author.
- Do a short presentation to the class about the author you have chosen.
- Write a short book review about each book using the book review sheet.

Ask the learners to open their books at page 36 and read through the rubrics.

This project will continue through to the following week so that you can listen to every learner give their oral presentation. Break up the project into sections and work out a time line for various sections to be handed in.

For example:

Day 3: Hand in the titles of three books by the same author that you have chosen.

Day 4: Be ready to do a short presentation to the class about the books you have chosen.

Day 8: Hand in book reviews on at least two books by the author you have chosen.

As each learner completes their presentation, let them add their author's name to a poster with the heading 'Authors'.

Extension: Learners draw the cover of one of the books they reviewed, including the title and author's name. Put these on the display board.

Weekly review

Use this rubric to assess learners' progress as they worked through the activities this week.

Level	Reading	Writing
■	This group needs guidance and support to choose an author and structure a reading project.	This group is beginning to vary the type of sentence they use but they still rely largely on simple and compound sentences for much of their writing work.
●	This group has begun to form opinions and can choose an author on their own, they may need some assistance planning and structuring their project.	This group varies their sentence types and are beginning to include complex sentences in their writing.
▲	This group can work independently to choose an author and can plan and structure their own project.	This group can confidently write with a variety of sentence types and use compound and complex sentences with confidence.

Week 3

Student's Book pages 37–39

Workbook pages 20–21

Student's Book pages 37-38

Writing

Ask the learners to turn to page 30 to the book review of *Oranges in No Man's Land* and ask them to read the first sentence out loud: 'Set in Lebanon during a civil war, this gripping story is about a ten-year-old girl called Ayesha and her journey to find a doctor and medicine for her grandmother.'

Ask the learners to read the first sentence of the last paragraph aloud: 'This is another wonderful book by an award-winning author.'

Ask: 'Which sentence is more interesting? Why?' (The first sentence is more interesting because it has lots of information about the book. It tells you *where* it takes place (Lebanon), *when* it takes place (civil war), *who* is in the story (a ten-year-old girl, Ayesha) and *what* the story is about (a journey to find a doctor and medicine.)) 'When you compare this with the other sentence does it make you want to read the book?' Discuss this.

Learners work in pairs and look at their reviews. They discuss whether they could make the first sentences of their reviews more interesting by changing some of the words by using synonyms, or by changing the order of the words of the first sentences. The learners revise the first sentence of each review.

While the learners are busy with this, walk around and support the pairs who are struggling to change the order of the words and, if necessary, suggest an appropriate synonym.

Spelling

Start the activity by writing some singular nouns on the board, for example: 'lady', 'lorry', 'pony', 'berry'.

Ask the learners to read the words aloud. Ask: 'What type of words are they? What is the same about all the words?' (They all end in *y*.) Ask if the nouns are referring to one or many. Explain that these nouns refer to one lady, one lorry, one pony, one berry. These nouns are 'singular', which means one. Write the word 'singular' on the board above the nouns. Explain that if there is more than one, it is called 'plural'. Write the word 'plural' on the board next to 'singular'. Point to the first word, 'lady', and say: 'one lady, many ladies'. Ask the learners what happens to the spelling of the noun if there is more than one. If they are unable to answer, write the word 'ladies' under the heading 'plural'. Repeat the question. The answer is: 'change the *y* to *i* and add –*es* to form the plural. Complete the rest of the words in the same manner.

Ask the learners to open their books at page 38 and read the teaching text to them. The learners read the rubric aloud together and complete the exercise.

Answers
a The stories about Ethiopia are in a book called *How the World Began*.
b Parties are great fun!
c Have you read the biographies of these authors?
d The babies are in the cribs.
e Which activities do you enjoy most?

Workbook page 20
Spelling
The learners complete the table of singular and plural nouns

Answers

Singular	Plural
country	countries
family	families
story	stories
orange	oranges
child	children
folktale	folktales
baby	babies
lady	ladies
diary	diaries
church	churches

Student's Book page 38
Writing
Before the lesson, prepare a letter to read to the class. Imagine that you are an author (choose one from the list of authors that the learners wrote on the poster), writing to the class. Mention that you (the author) have heard that the learners had been writing book reviews. Add some interesting information in the letter and maybe a question. Place the letter in an envelope, address it to the class and ask another teacher to deliver it to the class.

The lesson starts with the letter being delivered to the class. Read the letter to the class. When you come to the sender's name, appear puzzled and wonder out aloud who this person is. Hopefully, a learner will recognise the name, if not, give the learners some clues such as: 'This person seems to know a lot about books, their name sounds so familiar.' When the sender of the letter has been identified, ask the learners what they would like to ask their favourite author. Give the learners time to share their questions with the class.

Ask the learners to open their books at page 38. Read the rubric and go through the format of the letter. The learners write their letter in their exercise books.

Student's Book page 39
Reading
1 Ask the learners to write down their definition of a bookworm. If they don't know, ask them to look it up in their dictionaries. Discuss their definitions.

2 The learners work in pairs and read the poem aloud. Remind them to use their dictionaries to look up unfamiliar words.

While the learners are busy with practising the poem, write some of the unfamiliar words on the board, for example: 'fate', 'bait', 'churn', 'loll', 'wend'.

Ask the learners to explain the meaning of the words. If they are unable to do so, they need to look up the words in their dictionaries. Go through the poem with the learners, encouraging them to explain what they understand about the meaning of the verses.

Explain to the learners that there are ways to improve their reading aloud skills.

Write the first verse of the poem on the board. Elicit from the learners which words should be emphasised, and underline them. Ask the learners to look at the poem for punctuation – what do they notice? (There are no full stops.) Explain that poems often do not have punctuation, so when you read a poem you need to emphasise words or pause at the end of a line. Ask the learners to read the first verse again. Ask where the pauses should be. Make a star where the learners suggest a pause.

Ask the class to read the first verse together again, emphasising the underlined words and pausing at the stars.

Read the notepad feature to the learners. They complete the exercise. Give the learners an opportunity to read the poem aloud to the rest of the class.

Workbook page 21

Reading

The learners read the poem *Bookworms* and answer the questions.

Answers
1 some worms become bait, some worms make silk; 2 fate – bait; eat – meat; wend – end; 3a they both start with 'l'; b 'loll' means to slouch, lie back; c it describes the way that a worm would 'read' a book

Weekly review

Use this rubric to assess learners' progress as they worked through the activities this week.

Level	Reading	Writing	Listening and speaking
■	This group reads at a slow pace, but still needs some support to interpret the punctuation and the mood of the text.	This group can identify some grammar mistakes. They need support to correct and improve the language of texts.	This group needs much repetition to recite a poem with expression and rhythm.
●	This group is reading with more expression and has a fair understanding towards correctly interpreting the mood of the text.	This group can identify most grammar mistakes. They are able, with some support, to correct and improve the language of texts.	This group needs some repetition to recite a poem with expression and rhythm.
▲	This group reads with expression and understanding, correctly interpreting the mood of the text.	This group can identify grammar mistakes. They are able correct and improve the language of texts.	This group is able to recite a poem with expression, rhythm and enjoyment.

Unit 5 Amazing journeys

Unit overview

This unit is an extension of Unit 4 with a focus on reading different types of non-fiction texts. The learners will research non-fiction texts to acquire information. In the first week the learners will learn to use the contents page, the index and glossary of a book. Suffixes and singular and plural nouns are revisited. In the second week the learners are given the opportunity to show off their acting ability. Planning and writing a story will have the learners using the internet and the library for research. The learners will be guided through the process by first writing a draft of their text, checking punctuation and by using spellcheck when typing up their drafts. At the start of the third week, the learners will read their stories to the rest of the class. They will read a non-fiction text in order to compose their own questions. The learners will practise the past tense of verbs and the use of pronouns. The unit ends with the learners using the knowledge gained from reading non-fiction texts to write a personal account.

Reading	Writing	Listening and speaking
3R01 Use effective strategies to tackle blending unfamiliar words to read, including sounding out, separating into syllables, using analogy, identifying known suffixes and prefixes, using context;	3W04 Use IT to write, edit and present work;	3SL2 Adapt tone of voice, use vocabulary and non-verbal features for different audiences;
	3W07 Write simple sentences, dictated by the teacher, from memory;	
	3W10 Make a record of information drawn from a text, e.g. by completing a chart;	3SL6 Practise to improve performance when reading aloud;
3R05 Read aloud with expression to engage the listener;	3Wa6 Establish purpose for writing, using features and style based on model texts;	3SL7 Begin to adapt movement to create a character in drama.
3R08 Locate information in a non-fiction text using a contents page and index;	3Wt2 Begin to organise writing in sections or paragraphs in extended stories;	
3Rx1 Answer questions with some reference to single points in a text;	3Wt3 Plan main points as a structure for story writing;	
3R09 Use IT sources to locate simple information;	3Wp1 Maintain accurate use of capital letters and full stops in showing sentences and check by reading own writing aloud;	
3R11 Locate books by classification;		
3Rx2 Scan a passage to find specific information and answer questions;	3Ws3 Learn rules for adding –ing, –ed, –s to verbs;	
3Ri1 Begin to infer meanings beyond the literal, e.g. about motives and character;	3WP9 Identify pronouns and understand their function in a sentence;	
3Ri2 Infer the meaning of unknown words from the context;	3Wp11 Understand pluralisation and use the terms 'singular' and 'plural';	
3Rw3 Consider the way that information is set out on a page and on a screen, e.g. lists, charts, bullet points;	3Ws1 Use effective strategies to tackle segmenting unfamiliar words to spell, including segmenting into individual sounds, separating into syllables, using analogy, identifying known suffixes and prefixes, applying known spelling rules, visual memory, mnemonics;	
3Rv1 Identify the main purpose of a text.	3Ws4 Extend earlier work on prefixes and suffixes.	

Related resources

- Audio files: *The Journey of Humpback Whales*; *Cuckoos*; *Captain Scott: Journey to the South Pole*
- Slideshow 5: Amazing journeys
- PCM 9: Cuckoos
- PCM 10: Reading information books

Introducing the unit

Show a variety of mixed-media pictures of green turtles, wildebeest, salmon fish, monarch butterflies, hippopotamus, arctic terns, humpback whale, an elephant and a world map. Arrange the pictures around the map on the display board. Make a heading or banner titled 'Amazing journeys', but do not put it on the display board. Go to the library and take out a selection of non-fiction books about animals and explorers. Try to include a book on whales.

When you start the unit, ask the learners what these animals have in common. Quite possibly they will not know. Point to the world map and tell them that the map has something to do with the animals. Single out the humpback whale and ask the learners where they would see this whale. Mark the areas on the map with a sticker or a flag: Antarctica, east coast of Australia, South Africa and so on.

Allow the learners to offer their opinions as to why whales move around. Ask for a word that would describe moving from one area to another. Words such as 'travel', 'trip', 'tour', 'voyage', 'journey' could be suggested. Introduce the heading or banner 'Amazing journeys' and add it to the display. Have a brief discussion about the other pictures on display and see if any of the learners know about other journeys that the animals make.

Finally, ask the learners what type of books would give them information about these animals (non-fiction books, which they will find in the library in the 500–599 section). Refer to a book that is on display and ask: 'Where would you find out what is in this book?' The contents page tells us about the main sections or chapters into which the book is divided. It also gives the page numbers. An index, which is at the back of the book, tells you where you can find information about particular ideas or subjects. A glossary explains the meanings of words. Tell the learners that they are going to find information in a non-fiction book.

Week 1

Student's Book pages 40–45

Workbook pages 22–24

Student's Book page 40

Reading

Ask the learners to read the teaching text aloud. Explain to them that they are going to use the contents page and index to answer the questions.

Answers
a There are five sections or chapters in this book.
b page 14
c A glossary explains the meanings of words that relate to the text.
d pages 8, 9, 16, 18, 19
e the story of a humpback whale from birth to death
f pages 9, 11, 12, 14, 16, 18

Workbook page 22

Reading

Explain to the learners that they are going to look at two different books, specifically at the contents pages, and answer the questions.

Answers
1 B is non-fiction
2 stories or fables
3 electricity
4 The Shepherd Boy
5 Book A, page 15
6 Book B, page 21

Student's Book pages 41–44

Vocabulary

1–2 Ask the learners to scan the text and to write down words that look unfamiliar. Then they look up the words in the glossary. Discuss any words and meanings that were unfamiliar to the learners.

Read the notepad feature to the learners.

Reading non-fiction
Before the learners start to read, ask them to read the headings aloud and give them time to look at the pictures.

Reading and writing
Ask the learners to read the text aloud with a partner. They can then answer the questions.

Answers
a Humpback whales are mammals.
b Each humpback whale has a different white, grey and black pattern under its tail.
c They may swim up to 800,000 kilometres.
d 5,600 kilometres
e It takes two to three months to swim back from Tonga to Antarctica.
f The water is warmer near Tonga and the calves have a better chance of survival.
g The humpback whale's food is mainly krill.
h The dangers are: strong currents, storms, getting caught in fishing nets or being hit by boats. (any two)

Workbook page 23
Reading
Ask the learners to read *The Journey of Humpback Whales* again. Explain that they are going to complete the life cycle diagram of the humpback whale using the sentences in the box.

Student's Book pages 44–45
Spelling
Write the following words on the board: 'teach', 'farm', 'colour', 'nature'.

Explain that the meaning of these words can be changed by adding something at the end of each word. Ask for suggestions, write the words on the board and underline the letters at the end.

teach<u>er</u>, farm<u>er</u>, colour<u>ful</u>, natur<u>al</u>

Explain that by adding letters onto the end of words, the words can become adjectives, verbs, nouns and adverbs. Tell the learners that the letters added on to the end are called 'suffixes'.

1 Ask the learners to open their books at page 44 and read the rubric to them. They complete the exercise.

Answers
A few answers below, there are many others.

Word	Suffix	Other words with the same suffix
warmer	–er	closer, smoother, layer, painter
roughly	–ly	honestly, safely, quietly

Say: 'Let's look at nouns again'. Elicit the definition of a noun from the learners. (A noun is the name of an object.) Explain that most nouns can form a plural by adding –s or –es, for example: 'book' – 'books', 'pen' – 'pens', 'eye' – 'eyes'. But some nouns have irregular plural forms.

Write the following nouns on the board: 'calf', 'child', 'baby', 'man', 'roof'. Ask the learners for the plural form of the nouns. Write them on the board: 'calves', 'children', 'babies', 'men', 'roofs' (or 'rooves').

2 Divide the learners into groups. Explain that they are going to have a quiz. They must choose the correct plural form for each of the words. Encourage them to use their dictionaries to check their answers. Which group will finish first and have all the answers correct?

Answers
a women; b countries; c halves; d knives; e children; f geese; g loaves; h mice; I teeth; j oxen

Workbook page 24
Vocabulary and spelling
The learners read the clues, make new words and complete the crossword.

Answers
Across:
1 mice
4 survival
6 teeth
7 roughly
8 knives
Down:
2 calves
3 loaves
4 sadly
5 warmer

Weekly review

Use this rubric to assess learners' progress as they worked through the activities this week.

Level	Reading	Writing
■	This group reads at a slower pace. They need support to understand the different headings where information can be found in non-fiction texts when using the contents and index pages.	This group answers questions quoting directly from the non-fiction text. They require support to write answers to indirect questions. They are starting to recognise and use suffixes and pronouns.
●	This group is able to read the contents and index pages, but relies on glossaries to have a better understanding of the language used in non-fiction texts.	This group answers questions in their own words. They require some support to write answers to indirect questions. They recognise and use suffixes and pronouns.
▲	This group is able to read with understanding the contents and index pages and is able to draw facts from non-fiction texts.	This group answers questions in their own words. They are able to answer most of the indirect questions without support. They recognise and use suffixes and pronouns.

Week 2

Student's Book pages 45–47

Workbook page 25

Student's Book page 45

Listening and speaking

1 Explain to the learners that they must listen carefully to the text that you are going to read to them. Tell them that they are going to complete an information sheet based on what they hear. Allow them to make notes in a mind-map format if they need to.

> **Cuckoos**
>
> Cuckoos are common birds that migrate between Africa and Europe. They usually arrive in Europe and Asia in Spring (mid-April to early May).
>
> Cuckoos have a crafty breeding strategy. Instead of building their own nest, they use the nests of other birds. These birds are called hosts. When a female cuckoo finds a suitable nest, and the hosts aren't looking, she removes one of their eggs and lays her own egg in its place. She then moves on to another host nest and lays another egg. The young cuckoos hatch after only 12 days and quickly push the hosts' eggs or babies out of the nests.
>
> The adult cuckoos leave around July, long before the start of winter. Young cuckoos leave about one month later, when they are fully fledged. They never see their parents. The cuckoos migrate south, across the Mediterranean Sea and the Sahara Desert to countries like Cameroon in Africa.

When you have finished reading the text, divide the learners into pairs and ask them to act out what the cuckoos do.

Hand out PCM 9 and ask the learners to work in pairs to complete the activities. They will need to remember what they have heard or compare notes with each other if they are unsure of any of the information.

Workbook page 25

Vocabulary and spelling

The learners think about the meaning of the words from the text that they listened to about cuckoos. They choose the best meaning for each word in bold print.

Answers
1 c; **2** b; **3** b

Student's Book pages 46–47

Plan and write a story

Go to the display board where you have put up the pictures of different animals and the world map. Tell the learners that there are many animals that migrate. Some animals have made amazing journeys because they wanted to reach a certain place. Talk about the following amazing journeys and refer to the map to show where the animals are from:

- green turtles that live in the sea around Brazil and travel to Ascension Island in the South Atlantic Ocean to lay their eggs
- the journeys made by huge herds of wildebeest every year when the Serengeti

area (Kenya, Africa) where they live becomes too dry
- the migrations of salmon fish from the ocean to fresh water to lay their eggs
- the migrations of monarch butterflies
- the journey of Huberta the hippo in South Africa
- the journey of Lin Wang, the old elephant, who travelled miles across Burma and China.

Explain to the learners that they are going to find out about one of these journeys and write a story about it.

Ask the learners to open their books at page 47 and read the steps aloud together.

Step 1: Use the internet or the library to find out about some of these journeys.

Step 2: Decide which journey you want to write about.

Step 3: Plan your text.
- How many sections or paragraphs will you have?
- Will you use headings? What will the headings be?
- Will you add pictures? Remember to write captions to go with the pictures.

Step 4: Draft your text.

Improve your text

Step 5: Now check your text and then improve it.
- Have you used capital letters and full stops?
- Type your text on a computer and use the spellcheck to check your spelling.
- Use letters in different sizes or colours to make the text more interesting.

Discuss a suitable length for the story (based on abilities) and tell the learners when it needs to be finished.

Extension: Ask the learners to complete PCM 10 to summarise what they found out from reading an information text. If they do not use books in the activity, then let them complete the form by referring to the article they read on the internet.

Weekly review

Use this rubric to assess learners' progress as they worked through the activities this week.

Level	Writing
■	This group is able to write a story using two paragraphs, but require support to group the facts together.
●	This group is able to write a story using two longer paragraphs, grouping the facts correctly.
▲	This group is able to write a story using two longer paragraphs and using compound sentences. The facts are grouped correctly and logically.

Week 3

Student's Book pages 47–51

Workbook pages 26–29

Student's Book pages 47–50

Speaking to an audience
Tell the learners that they will have the opportunity to present their stories to the class. They must explain why they chose their story. Ask them to read the tips in the Student's Book.

Reading
Note: Please be aware that the text about Captain Scott ends tragically as the explorer and his party all perish on their return journey. You may need to treat this sensitively, depending on your class. Prepare learners for the ending if you think it may upset them.

1 Divide the learners into groups. Ask them to discuss and answer the questions before they read the text. Remind them to use their dictionaries if they are not sure of the meanings of words.

Answers
1a An explorer is a person who travels to new places.
b Antarctica is near the South Pole.
c A base camp is a place which is the centre of an operation.
d A sledge is a vehicle pulled by animals which transports people and goods across snow or ice.

2–3 The learners work with a partner and read the text together. When they are finished, they compile a list of six questions about the text. They must write down the questions and answers in their exercise books.

Support: Circulate while the learners are busy. Offer support with the type of questions, remind the learners to use question marks at the end of their questions.

4 Divide the learners into groups so that they can take turns to ask their questions. They see which pair in each group can answer the most questions correctly.

Workbook page 26
Reading and understanding
Ask the learners to read the story *Captain Scott: Journey to the South Pole* again. They circle the correct letters of the words to complete each sentence.

Answers
1 b
2 a
3 a
4 a
5 b

Student's Book page 51
Spelling
Revise verbs with the learners. Write some verbs on the board. Ask the learners to give you some examples of verbs, and write these on the board too.

Examples: jump, fetch, laugh.

Explain that these verbs are in the present tense. Ask the learners to change the verbs to the past tense ('jumped', 'fetched', 'laughed').

Ask the learners to write the paragraph in the past tense in their exercise books. Explain that the verbs are in brackets.

Answers
wanted, needed, pulled, arrived, reached

Workbook page 27
Grammar
The learners must find the verbs in the sentences, underline them then write the sentences in the past tense.

Answers
1 The whales <u>play</u> in the water with their calves.
The whales played in the water with their calves.
2 The cuckoo <u>pushes</u> an egg out of the host nest.
The cuckoo pushed an egg out of the host nest.
3 The hippo <u>lives</u> in a river in Zambia.
The hippo lived in a river in Zambia.
4 Scott <u>arrives</u> at the South Pole after Amundsen.
Scott arrived at the South Pole after Amundsen.
5 The whales <u>migrate</u> from colder places to warmer places.
The whales migrated from colder places to warmer places.
6 The humpbacks in the bay yesterday all <u>look</u> the same to me.
The humpbacks in the bay yesterday all looked the same to me.

Student's Book page 51
Grammar
Revise pronouns with the learners. Ask them to define a pronoun. A pronoun takes the place of a common noun (name of an object) or a proper noun (person's name). Divide the learners into pairs to discuss how to use a pronoun instead of the underlined words in each sentence. Read the sentences with the pronouns aloud.

Answers
a Scott's boat – It; **b** the dogs –them; **c** the men – they; **d** Mario and Pedro – They, their; **e** the cuckoos – they

Writing
Discuss the story of Captain Scott with the learners. Ask them to try and imagine how Captain Scott must have felt when he reached

the South Pole. Allow the learners some time to give their opinions. Ask them to imagine that they are Captain Scott and write a description of the day that you reached the South Pole.

Have the learners look in their books for an idea on how to start writing the personal account.

Workbook pages 28–29

Writing

1 Ask the learners to read through the notes and look at the map of the journeys of the green turtles. Tell them that they are going to use the information to write two paragraphs about the journeys of the green turtles.

2 When the learners have finished writing, instruct them to read the rubric on how to improve their writing. The learners make the necessary changes.

Weekly review

Use this rubric to assess learners' progress as they worked through the activities this week.

Level	Reading	Listening and speaking
■	This group need repeated practice to improve their reading performance.	This group is able, with support and demonstration, to adapt tone of voice and requires support to use the vocabulary relevant to the topics. They require encouragement to adapt a movement to create a character.
●	This group practise to improve their reading performance.	This group is able, with some support, to adapt tone of voice and mostly uses vocabulary relevant to the topics. They are generally able to adapt a movement to create a character.
▲	This group is able to read confidently both silently and aloud.	This group is able to adapt tone of voice, understands and uses vocabulary relevant to the topics. They are able to adapt a movement to create a character.

Unit 6 Myths and legends

Unit overview

The learners enter the world of fantasy and enchantment when they are introduced to myths and legends. They will read widely and infer meanings beyond what is in the text. In the first week the learners read a myth and answer questions which require much discussion. Dialogue between characters is addressed. Legends are the focus in the second week and the learners will be required to use the internet to find out some more information about the two legends. Adverbs and adverbial phrases are taught. The learners will experience the format of a play and have the opportunity to act out their play. In the third week another myth, in the form of a fable, will be read and discussed. The learners will have the opportunity to write their own myths. The past tense of irregular verbs is the focus for spelling and grammar.

There will be many opportunities during this unit for the teacher to assess the learners with regards to listening and speaking, inferring meanings beyond the literal, adapting movement to create a character and writing simple playscripts based on reading.

Reading	Writing	Listening and speaking
3R01 Use effective strategies to tackle blending unfamiliar words to read, including sounding out, separating into syllables, using analogy, identifying known suffixes and prefixes, using context;	3W06 Use reading as a model for writing dialogue;	3SL3 Take turns in discussion, building on what others have said;
	3W07 Write simple sentences, dictated by the teacher, from memory;	3SL4 Listen and respond appropriately to others' views and opinions;
	3W08 Write simple playscripts based on reading;	
3R02 Read a range of story, poetry and information books and begin to make links between them;	3Wa1 Develop descriptions of settings in stories;	3SL6 Practise to improve performance when reading aloud;
	3Wa4 Explore vocabulary for introducing and concluding dialogue, e.g. 'said', 'asked';	3SL7 Begin to adapt movement to create a character in drama.
3R06 Sustain the reading of 48–64 page books, noting how a text is organised into sections or chapters;	3Wa5 Generate synonyms for high frequency words, e.g. 'big', 'little', 'good';	
3R07 Use knowledge of punctuation and grammar to read age-appropriate texts with fluency, understanding and expression;	3Wa6 Establish purpose for writing, using features and style based on model texts;	
3R09 Use IT sources to locate simple information;	3Wa7 Write first-person accounts and descriptions based on observation;	
3R12 Read playscripts and dialogue, with awareness of different voices;	3Wt1 Develop range of adverbials to signal the relationship between events;	
3Rx1 Answer questions with some reference to single points in a text;	Continue to improve consistency in the use of tenses;	
3Rx2 Scan a passage to find specific information and answer questions;	3Wt2 Begin to organise writing in sections or paragraphs in extended stories;	
3Rx3 Identify the main points or gist of a text;	3Wt3 Plan main points as a structure for story writing;	
3Rv3 Identify different types of stories and typical story themes;	3Wp6 Learn the basic conventions of speech punctuation and begin to use speech marks;	
3Ri1 Begin to infer meanings beyond the literal, e.g. about motives and character.	3Wp12 Know irregular forms of common verbs.	

Related resources:

- Audio files: *The Legend of Achilles*; *The Legend of the Queen of Sheba*; *The Wind and the Sun*
- Slideshow 6: Myths and legends
- PCM 11: Australian animals
- PCM 12: What is the question?
- PCM 13: Describing characters

Introducing the unit

Find some pictures of the following animals that appear in the first story. Do not display them, but keep them for the discussion that will take place after the learners have read the story of *Tiddalik the Frog*: frog, wombat, kangaroo, kookaburra, lizard, emu, eel.

Make a banner with the word 'Myths' and another with 'Legends' and put them on the display board. Source some books from the library to form part of the display.

Start the lesson by asking the learners who can explain what the two words mean. Ask: 'What are the differences between a myth and a legend?' Allow enough time for discussion.

Show the various book covers. Spend some time talking about what each book is likely to be about.

Week 1

Student's Book pages 52–56

Workbook pages 30–31

Student's Book pages 52–55

Reading and speaking

1 Ask the learners to open their books and read the definitions aloud together. Ask the learners to try to read the definitions on their own before you read them aloud. Discuss the definitions with the class. Refer back to the images you used in the warm up and ask the learners to classify these as myths or legends.

Spend some time discussing the questions with the class. Make sure they understand and can express the difference between a myth and a legend.

As learners identify mythical creatures, record their suggestions (these can be used as a starting point for role-playing characters and work art lessons). Some examples the learners may know are: mermaids, abominable snowman (yeti), amarok, Cyclops, gremlins, kelpies, kraken, Loch Ness monster, Nyami-nyami, ogres, orcs, Pegasus, phoenix, trolls and unicorns. If they don't know any, you could turn this into a research task by displaying the names and asking the learners to find out what these are.

Ask: 'Do you know any legends?' Allow the learners to talk freely about what they perceive is a legend. Here are some examples of legends: King Arthur, Robin Hood, Aladdin.

Ask the learners to read the definitions again.

Workbook page 30

Reading and thinking

The learners read the sentences and circle the word that has a similar meaning to the word in bold.

Answers
1 deeds
2 really
3 imaginary
4 over-state
5 believable

Student's Book pages 52–55

Reading and speaking

2 Tell the class that you are going to read the story of *Tiddalik the Frog*. Before you start, tell them that the story is set in Australia, show the class the map of the world and identify Australia. Let the class share what they know about Australia.

Discuss the word 'Aboriginal'. Tell learners that 'Aboriginal' refers to the Aboriginal people of Australia. The Aboriginals are an indigenous community that respect the land which is fundamental to their wellbeing. They have understood and cared for different environments and have adapted to them.

The Dreamtime stories are the Aboriginal equivalent of 'once upon a time' stories that explain how the earth as we know it came to be.

Let the learners skim the story and look at the pictures to familiarise themselves with it.

Next, let the learners read the story silently. If they don't know the meaning of a word, ask them to write it down. Discuss the meanings as a class if necessary.

Once the learners have read the text silently, ask them if there are any words they cannot pronounce. Use phonics to sound out the words and practise saying them aloud before moving on.

Read the story aloud to the class to reinforce both the story and the pronunciation, and ask the learners to follow in their books.

Let the learners answer the questions about the story in small groups or pairs. Show the pictures that you sourced before starting the unit.

Answers
2a It is a myth because the animals talk in the story.
b The main character is Tiddalik the frog, and the other characters are: a wombat, a kangaroo, a kookaburra, lizards, emus and an eel.
c The story is set in the Australian outback. Discuss what is meant by the outback.
d Ask the learners for the words that they do not know. Ask them to take out their dictionaries and look up the words and discuss the meanings.

Student's Book page 55
Reading and speaking
1 Ask the learners to read the story *Tiddalik the Frog* again. Go over the meanings of the unfamiliar words. Ask them to work with a partner to answer the questions.

Answers
1a Australia
b outback, dry, water hole
c Tiddalik drank all the water in the water hole, stream, lake, all the water everywhere.
d The trees and grasses withered and flopped over. The animals searched for water, they would soon die of thirst.
e The wombat suggested that they must make Tiddalik laugh then he would open his mouth wide and the water will flow out.
f The kookaburra told his best jokes in his loudest voice.
g The eel made Tiddalik laugh. The sand was so hot that he couldn't crawl over it, so he tried to stand up on the end of his tail, but he was unable to balance and bent himself in all sorts of shapes.

Extension: Ask the learners to imagine that they are an eel and to demonstrate how the eel tried to balance on the end of its tail.

Before starting the next section of questions, ask the learners to look at a map of Australia. Ask questions that would lead them to understand that most of Australia is a desert region, for example: 'Are there many rivers in the centre of Australia? What type of vegetation do you think would grow there? What type of farming would take place there? How would you describe the central area of Australia?'

2 Divide the learners into small groups to answer the questions.

Give the learners enough time to answer the questions. The following questions should be discussed as a class:

- Why do you think the Aboriginal people told this story? (to show respect for water)
- What does this myth teach us about sharing and fairness? (there is enough for everyone)
- Why do you think the animals tried to make the frog laugh rather than hurting him to spill the water? (If they hurt the frog, he might swallow the water then no one will have water. Also, the Aboriginal Dreamtime stories rely on respect for all living creatures, so they would not harm one creature, even if it behaves badly.)

Student's Book page 56
Reading and speaking
Ask the learners how they can identify dialogue in a story. (Dialogue is always in speech marks.) The speech marks are the words that a character said.

Ask the learners to look at *Tiddalik the Frog*. Explain that they going to find the dialogue in the story. Pretend to be the character who speaks the words. Read the dialogue with expression.

Use this section to evaluate learners' speaking skills whilst moving from group to group.

Hand out PCM 12 and ask the learners to read the answers in the speech bubbles. In pairs, ask the learners to discuss then write down what the question might have been in each case.

Workbook pages 30–31
Reading comprehension
Ask the learners to read the story *Tiddalik the Frog* again and answer the questions.

Answers
1 a wombat; **b** Tiddalik; **c** kookaburra;
d kangaroo; **e** eel
2 Plants and animals need water to survive. When Tiddalik laughed, the water flowed out of his mouth.

Grammar
Learners write these verbs in the past tense.

Answers
complain – complained   hop – hopped
move – moved   search – searched

Student's Book page 56

Vocabulary

1 Explain to the learners that in the story about Tiddalik, the author used dialogue, but he did not always use the words 'said' or 'asked'. They must find seven words that he author used instead of 'said'.

2 Learners copy the dialogues into their exercise books. They use synonyms for 'said'.

Answers
a complained
b muttered
c cried
d moaned
e shouted
f laughed

Workbook page 31

Vocabulary

The learners read the definitions, write the name of each animal and draw a line to match it to the correct definition.

Answers
a long snake-like fish: eel
a large flightless bird: emu
an animal with webbed feet, moist skin and strong back legs for jumping: frog
an animal with large back feet, fur and strong back legs for jumping: kangaroo
a small furry animal that looks like a bear: wombat

Use PCM 11 to consolidate work on finding information in a resource book and to prepare a sheet about Australian animals which do not appear in the story.

Weekly review

Use this rubric to assess learners' progress as they worked through the activities this week.

Level	Reading	Writing	Listening and speaking
■	This group is starting to read with expression and enjoyment. They are able to scan the text, but require some support to find specific information to answer questions.	This group answers questions quoting directly from the text. They require some support to write answers to indirect questions.	This group is able, with support and demonstration, to read dialogue with awareness of different voices.
●	This group can for the most part read with enjoyment and expression. They are better at scanning the text to find specific information to answer questions.	This group answers questions in their own words. They are better at answering indirect questions.	This group is able, with some support, to read dialogue with awareness of different voices.
▲	This group reads with enjoyment and expression. They are able to scan the text to find specific information to answer questions with ease.	This group answers questions in their own words. They are able to answer most of the indirect questions without support.	This group is able to read dialogue with awareness of different voices.

Week 2

Student's Book pages 57–60

Workbook page 32

Student's Book page 57

Grammar

Start the lesson by reviewing verbs. Ask:' What is a verb?' (It is an action word.) Ask for some examples of verbs. Ask the learners to look at the verbs in the story *Tiddalik the Frog*: 'woke', 'lap', 'drank', 'see', 'hopped' and so on.

Explain that they are going to look at words that help verbs. These words tell us *how* the action is done or carried out, and are called 'adverbs'. On the board write a heading 'verb' and a heading 'adverb'.

Write 'walk' under 'verb'. Ask the learners to think of a word that would tell you *how* someone walked. As the learners give you words, write them under the 'adverb' heading, for example: 'slowly', 'quickly', 'speedily' and so on. Put the verb and adverb in a sentence, for example: 'Please walk slowly down the hill.' Discuss the word 'slowly'. It tells us more about the verb 'walk'. It tells us how you must walk down the hill. Repeat the definition of an adverb: adverbs tell us how the action is done or carried out.

Explain 'adverbial phrases'. An adverbial phrase is a group of words that tell us more about verbs.

Example: Later in the afternoon, an eel wiggled out from under his sleeping rock.

Ask: 'What is the verb in the sentence?' (wiggled) 'Which group of words tells us *when* the eel wiggled?' (later in the afternoon) Say: 'We call this group of words an adverbial phrase.'

Ask the learners to open their books at page 57. Read the teaching text together. Explain that they are going to copy the paragraph into their exercise books, and choose an adverb or an adverbial phrase from the box to complete each sentence. Ask the learners to read the words in the box.

Answers
Tiddalik drank till the water hole was dry. **After that** Tiddalik was much fatter than before, but he was still thirsty. **By night-time** Tiddalik had drunk all the water in the land. **The following day** all the animals were very worried. They made a plan. They decided that they would try to make Tiddalik laugh and open his mouth wide. After **several performances** Tiddalik had still done nothing but blink. **Finally** the eel crept out and danced. **At last** Tiddalik laughed and all the water came out of his mouth. **Happily** there was now enough water for all the animals again.

Workbook page 32

Writing
Ask the learners to look at the picture. Explain that they are going to use the information to write a description of the possum.

Student's Book page 58

Reading and writing
1 Discuss 'a play' with the learners. Find out if anyone has been to a concert. Ask about the type of concert: 'Were people or children dancing, or singing, or playing musical instruments or were there people or children pretending to be someone else in a story?' A play is a performance, a theatrical production, a show. Everyone in a play has words and sentences to say to another person, called 'dialogue'. Explain to the learners that they are going to work in groups and turn the story of Tiddalik into a play.

Ask the learners to open their books and to look at the example. Ask them to scan the text. Ask: 'What do you notice about the text?' Answer: Some of the text is in italics and some words are written in bold.

Read through the text of Scene 1 while the learners follow in their books. When you have finished reading Scene 1 ask the learners if they can explain why some of the text is written in italics.

The parts written in italics are telling the character or actors where they need to stand, or what they need to do while someone is speaking. The words written in bold are the names of the characters or actors.

Read Scene 1 again, this time the learners read the italics only and you read the role of Tiddalik. Repeat this, but with the learners reading Tiddalik and you reading the italics.

Ask the learners to look at the notepad text about how characters move. Read the note aloud together.

Divide the learners into groups and they write a short play together. While they are busy with this, walk around and support where needed. Encourage the learners to refer back to the story for ideas and to check who said what.

When the learners have completed writing the play, give them time to read the play. Each learner in a group is a specific character. Allow them to make adjustments.

2 Allow the learners to practise their play using actions and movements to demonstrate the characters in the story. Give each group the opportunity to perform their play for the others.

Student's Book pages 59–60

Reading
Explain to the learners that they are going to read two famous legends. Allow them to read *The Legend of Achilles* quietly to themselves, then read the story aloud to them as they listen. Discuss the questions on Student's Book page 59 with the learners.

Then ask the learners read *The Legend of the Queen of Sheba* quietly to themselves, then out aloud together. Discuss the questions on Student's Book page 59 together.

Answers
1a Achilles, Helen, Paris, Hector; the Queen of Sheba, King Solomon
b *The Legend of Achilles* is set in the city of Troy more than 3000 years ago; *The Legend of the Queen of Sheba* is set in an ancient kingdom called Sheba during the 10th century.
c Achilles was a great warrior. He helped the Greeks to win the war. It seemed that he could not be killed in battle. His motive was to rescue Helen. Paris killed Achilles because it seemed that Achilles could not be killed in battle, he was invincible; The Queen of Sheba King Solomon was very wise and the Queen of Sheba wanted to find out more about him.
d The two main characters are historically real. It is possible that the Queen of Sheba went to visit King Solomon, but we don't know if she went there to test his wisdom.

2 Tell the learners that they need to use the internet or library to find the answers to the questions.

Workbook page 32
Reading and understanding
Ask the learners to read *The Legend of Achilles* again and to answer the questions.

Answers
1 Achilles' mother was Thetis, a nymph, and his father was Pelus, a king.
2 Achilles lived in ancient Greece more than 3,000 years ago.
3 He fought in the Trojan War.
4 Helen
5 Hector
6 Paris shot Achilles in the heel with an arrow.
7 An 'Achilles heel' means an area of weakness. His mother held him by his heel when she dipped him in the sacred water to protect him from injury. This part of his foot was not dipped into the water and therefore was not protected.

Student's Book page 60
Writing
Explain to the learners that they are going to find out some more about the Queen of Sheba using the internet. Ask them to imagine that they travelled with the Queen. The learners write a diary entry about a day or an event during the trip.

Weekly review
Use this rubric to assess learners' progress as they worked through the activities this week.

Level	Reading	Writing	Listening and speaking
■	This group needs support to make links between stories and to infer meanings from texts. They need support to source information when using the internet.	This group is able to identify adverbs, but require support with adverbial phrases. They use paragraphs and, with support, include some dialogue when writing a story. They need support to understand the format of a simple playscript.	This group is beginning to adapt a movement to create a character in drama.
●	This group is able to make some links between stories and needs support to infer meanings from texts. They are able to source information when using the internet, but not all is relevant.	This group is mostly able to correctly identify and use adverbial phrases. They use paragraphs and include some dialogue when writing a story. They have a fair understanding of the format of a simple playscript.	This group is able, with some support, to adapt a movement to create a character in drama.
▲	This group is able to make links between stories and is able to infer meanings from texts. They are able to source relevant information when using the internet.	This group correctly identifies and uses adverbial phrases. They use paragraphs and dialogue when writing a story. They have a good understanding of the format of a simple playscript.	This group is able to adapt a movement to create a character in drama.

Week 3

Student's Book pages 61–62

Workbook pages 33–35

Student's Book page 61

Spelling and grammar

Revise verbs with the learners. Look at irregular verbs again. Explain that some verbs change completely when they are written in the past tense; they are called 'irregular verbs'.

Read the notepad to the learners.

Explain to the learners that they going to write the sentences in the past tense in their exercise books. They must change the verb in brackets in each sentence.

Answers
a became; **b** drank; **c** told; **d** felt; **e** shone, rained; **f** thought, went

Workbook page 33

Spelling and grammar

Ask the learners find the irregular past tense forms of the verbs in the word puzzle. They write the words in the chart.

Answers

Present tense	Past tense
become	became
drink	drank
know	knew
blow	blew
think	thought
tell	told
see	saw
buy	bought
fly	flew
are	were
fall	fell

Student's Book pages 61–62

Reading

1–2 The learners read the myth *The Wind and the Sun* by themselves and answer the questions that follow.

Answers
2a The main characters are the wind and the sun.
b They argued about who was the strongest and the most important.
c The characters decided to have a competition.
d The sun won the competition.
e The wind was angry.
f Gentle persuasion is stronger than force.

Workbook page 34

Vocabulary and writing

1 Ask the learners to look up the adjectives in their dictionaries and choose the correct meaning for each word.

2 The learners use the words to write a short description of the characters of the sun and the wind in the story *The Wind and the Sun*.

Answers
a boastful: talk about yourself in a way that is very proud
b stubborn: determined not to change ideas about something

2 Explain to the learners that they are going to use the two words to write a short description of the characters of the sun and the wind in the story.

Student's Book page 62

Writing

Explain to the learners that they are going to write their own myth in the same style as the *The Sun and The Wind*. Ask them to read the points in the Student's Book.

Remind the learners that the setting of a story is the place where the story occurs, but it is also the time when the story occurs. Give them examples that they could use to describe the setting of a myth:

Once upon a time …

Long, long ago …

A long time ago …

Workbook page 35

Writing

1 Explain to the learners that they are going to replace the word 'said' in the story of *The Lion and the Mouse* with more interesting words from the box.

Answers
"I am going to eat you!" **roared** Lion.
"Please do not eat me," **begged** Mouse.
"And why not?" questioned Lion.
"Maybe I can help you one day," **squeaked** Mouse. Lion laughed long and heartily at this.
"Please explain how a tiny mouse like you could possibly help me," **sneered** Lion.

2 Ask the learners to read the myth *The Wind and The Sun* again. They look for the dialogue in the story and write the story as a short play.

Hand out PCM 13 to the learners and ask them to complete it independently. Use their written work to assess informally how well they understand the concept of a character, if they can write a description and given reasons for their choices.

Weekly review
Use this rubric to assess learners' progress as they worked through the activities this week.

Level	Writing
■	This group is able to use paragraphs and, with support, include some dialogue when writing a story.
●	This group is mostly able to use paragraphs and include some dialogue when writing a story.
▲	This group correctly uses paragraphs and dialogue when writing a story.

Formal assessment 2 Units 4–6
Use the test on pages 115–119 to assess how well the learners have managed to cover the objectives from units 4 to 6. Hand out the sheets and let the learners complete them under test conditions. Collect and mark their tests, recording the results in your class record book. Take note of any weak areas that you may need to revisit over the next few lessons.

Use the mark scheme below.

Total 40

Question 1
Reading (9)
A The text is a myth because one of the characters is a mythical creature (Minotaur). (2)

B Theseus, Princess Ariadne (2)

C Princess Ariadne helped Theseus because she had fallen in love with him. (1) He promised to take her back to Athens. (1)

D The ball of thread helped Theseus to find his way out of the labyrinth/maze. (2)

E Theseus' father saw white sails. (1)

Question 2
Grammar and vocabulary (13)
A Plural form (3)

children

these

sails

B Fill in adverbs or adverbial phrases in the text. (3)

Seven boys and girls were sent <u>into the maze</u> to be eaten alive.

Theseus promised his father that he was coming back <u>alive</u>.

Princess Ariadne said: "Hide these inside the <u>entrance to the maze</u>. "

C Join the two sentences to make a compound sentences.

Theseus heard a loud roar. The Minotaur charged.

Theseus heard a loud roar <u>and</u> the Minotaur charged. (2)

You must wait until the gate is closed. Tie the one end of the thread to the door of the labyrinth.

You must wait until the gate is closed <u>then</u> <u>tie</u> one end of the thread to the door of the labyrinth. (2)

D Use synonyms instead of 'said'. (3)

"I will return," <u>promised</u> Theseus to his father.

"What colour are the sails?" <u>asked</u> the king.

"I will kill the Minotaur!" <u>shouted</u> / <u>yelled</u> / <u>cried</u> / <u>exclaimed</u> Theseus.

Question 3

Writing (15)

Allow the learners to be creative for this exercise as long as they stick to the basic idea of the story. The following is an example of possible answers.

Scene 1

A ship arrives in the bay of Crete. Princess Ariadne sees Theseus.

Princess Ariadne: Who is the handsome young man from Crete? He looks very strong. (2)

Theseus: I have been sent to be eaten by the Minotaur. (2)

Scene 2

Princess Ariadne meets Theseus before he enters the maze.

Princess Ariadne: I can help you. Use the ball of thread to help you find your way out of the maze. (1) Tie the thread to the door and unravel it as you move through the maze. (1) Here is a sword to kill the Minotaur. (1) You must promise to take me with you when you leave Crete. (1)

Theseus: I am so grateful! I will follow your advice and if I am successful, I promise to take you with me. (2)

Scene 3

Theseus kills the Minotaur and leaves Crete with Princess Ariadne.

Spelling and grammar

1–3 spelling and grammar mistakes (3)

4–6 spelling and grammar mistakes (2)

7 or more spelling and grammar mistakes (1)

Content

2 marks for relevant, coherent dialogue

B Write down the names of two other myths or legends that you know. (2)

Tiddalik the Frog / The Sun and the Wind / The Legend of Achilles / Robin Hood (any 2)

C Using the Dewey Decimal Classification system, where in the library would you find books on myths and legends? 800–899 (1)

Unit 7 On stage

Unit overview

In Unit 6 the learners were introduced to the format of a playscript. In this unit the main focus is on reading, writing and acting out a playscript. In the first week the learners will listen to a story, study the characters and act the story. They are introduced to props and will follow instructions to make their own. In the second week the learners read a playscript. They come to understand how instructions are given to actors in a play. Using the playscript the learners write a character portrait. Grammar includes noun phrases and apostrophes. In the third week the learners use all the skills taught in the first two weeks to write a short playscript and perform their play for the class. The unit ends with a poem that has dialogue and strong descriptive phrases.

Reading	Writing	Listening and speaking
3R02 Read a range of story, poetry and information books and begin to make links between them;	3W07 Write simple sentences, dictated by the teacher, from memory;	3SL1 Speak clearly and confidently in a range of contexts, including longer speaking turns;
3R05 Read aloud with expression to engage the listener;	3Wa10 Write letters, notes and messages;	3SL2 Adapt tone of voice, use of vocabulary and non-verbal features for different audiences;
3R10 Read and follow instructions to carry out an activity;	3Wa2 Write portraits of characters;	3SL6 Practise to improve performance when reading aloud;
3R12 Read playscripts and dialogue, with awareness of different voices;	3Wa3 Choose and compare words to strengthen the impact of writing, including noun phrases;	3SL7 Begin to adapt movement to create a character in drama.
3Rx3 Identify the main points or gist of a text;	3Wa4 Explore vocabulary for introducing and concluding dialogue, e.g. 'said', 'asked';	
3Ri2 Infer the meaning of unknown words from the context;	3Wa6 Establish purpose for writing, using features and style based on model texts;	
3Rw2 Consider words that make an impact e.g. adjectives and powerful verbs.	3Wp5 Recognise the use of the apostrophe to mark omission in shortened words, e.g. 'can't', 'don't';	
	3Wp8 Collect examples of nouns, verbs, and adjectives, and use the terms appropriately.	

Related resources

- Audio files: *Chicken Licken*; *The Stone Cutter*
- Slideshow 7: On stage
- PCM 14: Grammar

Introducing the unit

Start this unit with a discussion about a movie that most of the learners have seen. Ask the learners to talk about the actors and the characters that they portrayed. Discuss the actors' actions and the scenery in the movie. Ask the learners how the actors know what to say and do. Lead the discussion so that the learners come to know that the actors have a script, which tells them how to say their lines and what actions they need to do. The actors portray a particular character in the movie, and sometimes, they need to change the colour of their hair, walk in a different way and talk using a different accent. Explain that in this unit, they are going to read playscripts and will write their own play.

Show the slideshow to the class and have them work in pairs to 'perform' the scene on each slide.

Week 1

Student's Book pages 63–64

Workbook pages 36–39

Student's Book pages 63–64

Listening and speaking

1–2 Tell the learners that you are going to read the story of *Chicken Licken* to them. Before you start reading, as the learners to look at the characters in the story. They must try to imagine how they would speak and move. They must listen carefully to the order in which things happen in the story. Read the story aloud to the class.

Chicken Licken by Jeremy Strong

Chicken Licken was taking a stroll when an acorn fell on his head.

PING!

"The sky is falling down!" he yelled. "I'd better tell the king."

He hurried off and soon met Henny Penny.

"Where are you going?" she clucked.

"The sky's falling down," panted Chicken Licken. "Got to tell the king!"

"Falling down? I'd better come with you," said Henny Penny.

They ran towards the palace and soon they met Cocky Locky.

"What are you two up to?" he asked.

"BIG trouble," said Henny Penny. "Chicken Licken says the sky's falling down and we're all going to DIE. We're going to tell the king."

Cocky Locky's eyes popped. "We'll all be CRUSHED! I'll come with you."

They set off to see the king, and who did they meet but Ducky Lucky.

(At this point, you could stop and let the pupils imagine what happened when the group met Cocky Locky, Drakey Lakey, Goosey Loosey and Turley Lurkey.)

"Where are you three going?" she quacked.

"I've just met Henny Penny," said Cocky Locky. "She met Chicken Licken, and he says the sky's falling down and the world is coming to an end and we shall all DIE!"

Ducky Lucky turned even whiter. "We'd better tell the king."

They turned the corner and almost ran down Drakey Lakey.

"What's the hurry?" he cried.

"The world's coming to an end," said Ducky Lucky. "Cocky Locky saw Henny Penny and Henny Penny saw Chicken Licken and he says the sky is falling down and we'll all get CRUSHED and DIE! We're going to tell the king, right now."

"But it's my birthday tomorrow," said Drakey Lakey. "I don't want the sky falling down. I'm coming with you."

A bit further on they bumped into Goosey Loosey.

"What's all the fuss?" she cried.

"End of the world!" moaned Drakey Lakey. "It's my birthday tomorrow! Ducky Lucky saw Cocky Locky who saw Henny Penny who saw Chicken Licken, and he says the sky's falling down and we're all going to get CRUSHED and DIE!"

Goosey Loosey honked in horror. "I don't want to die. The king must do something."

They all scurried off towards town and soon met Gander Lander.

Goosey Loosey told Gander Lander everything. "End of the world," she wailed. "Drakey Lakey saw Ducky Lucky and she saw Cocky Locky and he saw Henny Penny and she saw Chicken Licken and he says the sky's falling down! We'll all be SQUASHED! We're going to tell the king."

"Right," frowned Gander Lander. "I'm coming with you."

They hurried along, not really looking where they were going, and bumped into Turkey Lurkey.

"What's going on here?" he demanded.

"We've got to see the king," said Gander Lander. "I met Goosey Loosey and Goosey Loosey met Drakey Lakey and Drakey Lakey met Ducky Lucky and Ducky Lucky met Cocky Locky and Cocky Locky met Henny Penny and Henny Penny met Chicken Licken and Chicken Licken says the sky's falling down and the world is coming to an end and we're all going to be SQUASHED and DIE!

Turkey Lurkey shrieked. "If *anyone* tells the king *anything*, it'll be *me*. Now LET'S GO!"

Running helter-skelter down the High Street, they met Foxy Loxy.

"Hello," he smiled.

All the birds gabbled at once and told Foxy Loxy the sky was falling down and they were all going to die.

"Really?" said Foxy Loxy.

"YES!" said Chicken Licken. "I was in the wood and a bit of the sky hit me on the head. We're going to tell the king."

"Oh dear," drawled Foxy Loxy. "That is bad news. Follow me. I'll show you the way."

So they followed Foxy Loxy to his den.

Into Foxy Loxy's den went Chicken Licken, Henny Penny, Cocky Locky, Ducky Lucky, Drakey Lakey, Goosey Loosey, Gander Lander and Turkey Lurkey …

And Foxy Loxy and his wife and children ate up every one of them.

The sky did not fall down. But Chicken Licken and his friends did all die ... and they did meet a king – the KING OF TRICKS!

3 Ask the learners to work in pairs and to retell the story to each other. Walk around and listen to the learners while they are busy.

4 Discuss the characters in the story. Ask:
- Who do you think is silly? (Chicken Licken because he thought that the sky fell on his head.)
- Who do you think is proud? (Drakey Lakey, because it was his birthday and he didn't want anything to spoil his day.)
- Who do you think is nervous? (Cocky Locky because he thought they would all be crushed.)
- Who do you think is clever? (Foxy Loxy because he knew that sky couldn't fall.)

Discuss the remaining questions with the learners:
- Do they think before they act?
- Do they all panic?
- Do they all follow what others do without thinking?
- How do you think the characters move and talk?

Support: Use PCM 14 to assess understanding of the story and to reinforce and consolidate some basic grammatical structures. Hand out the sheets and let learners work first in pairs to discuss and complete the work orally before asking them to do the task in writing on their own.

Workbook page 36

Listening and understanding

1 Read the story of *Chicken Licken* again. The learners answer the questions, using complete (full) sentences.

2 Ask the learners to fill in the missing words from the box to match the story.

Answers
1a Chicken Licken thought the sky was falling down because he felt something fall on his head.
b Chicken Licken was walking outside when it happened.
c Chicken Licken wanted to tell the king.
d Foxy Loxy was the last animal that Chicken Licken met.
2 acorn, down, king, met, palace, Foxy, den

Workbook page 37

Grammar

1 The learners circle the correct word in each sentence.

2 The learners fill in the blanks with the correct form of the word in brackets.

Answers
1 is, are, is, were, was
2 taking, said, die, went, ate

Student's Book page 64

Listening and speaking (continued)

5 Divide the learners into groups of nine to act out the story of *Chicken Licken*. For them to do this, they must consider what kind of animals they are, how the animals would talk and how the animals would move.

Workbook page 38

Vocabulary

Explain to the learners that they are going to use synonyms to replace the words 'said' and 'asked' in the sentences.

Answers
a quacked
b honked

c drawled
d wailed
e demanded

Writing

Ask the learners to write a different ending for the story of *Chicken Licken*. They must use complete sentences. Depending on the learner's ability, it may be necessary to have a discussion about different endings prior to the independent writing.

Student's Book page 64

Reading instructions

1 Discuss props with the learners. Explain that the word 'props' means anything that you would use in a play to help the audience understand the play. A prop could be a mask, a costume or a piece of furniture. They could make masks or name tags for each character. Ask them to read the instructions about how to make a mask as a prop to use in a play. The learners make a mask and use it to act out the story of *Chicken Licken*.

Workbook page 39

Reading instructions

Ask the learners to open their books and read the instructions aloud.

Answers
How to make a paper tree
You will need:
a few sheets of newspaper
scissors and an elastic band
an acorn (or small round object) to hang on the tree
What you do:
First put the sheets on top of each other.
Roll the sheets up into a tube.
Tie the elastic band around the tube.
Cut some long slits in the paper.
Cut from the top and cut about a quarter of the way down.
Pull the middle of the tube up and out.
Hang the acorn on the tree.

Student's Book page 64

Listening and speaking (continued)

5 Now that the learners have made some props, allow sufficient time for the groups to practice. Each group acts out the story of *Chicken Licken*.

Weekly review

Use this rubric to assess learners' progress as they worked through the activities this week.

Level	Writing	Listening and speaking
■	This group correctly identifies nouns, but requires support to identify and use noun phrases. They use some of the features relevant to the writing of playscripts. They have a basic understanding of the format of a simple playscript.	This group needs support and guidance to sustain focus in a longer listening task.
●	This group correctly identifies nouns and uses some noun phrases when writing a playscript. They use most of the features relevant to the writing of playscripts. They have a fair understanding of the format of a simple playscript.	This group are mostly able to sustain their focus in a longer listening task.
▲	This group correctly identifies and uses noun phrases when writing a playscript. They use features relevant to the writing of playscripts. They have a good understanding of the format of a simple playscript.	This group find it easy to maintain a good focus during a longer listening task.

Week 2

Student's Book pages 65–70

Workbook pages 40–41

Student's Book pages 65–69

Reading a playscript

1 Before starting this play, have some pictures of rhinos to show the learners. It would be useful to have some facts ready, such as: numbers of rhinos in the world, how many are killed per month, why are they killed, etc.

Ask the learners to share what they know about rhinos. Add to their information using the facts that you researched.

2 Ask the learners to open their books and read the information about rhinos.

Explain that they are going to read a play. Ask them to read aloud the setting and the characters in the play. Discuss the different animals in the play, and ask the learners to look at the pictures.

3 Explain the use of italic print in the play. Read the notepad explanation to the learners.

Divide the learners into groups: rhinos, hippos, giraffes. Each group reads their part. You beat the drum for the first reading of the play.

After the first reading of the play *Going … Going …*, encourage the learners to offer their opinions. Ask whether the beating of the drum helped in any way. What did they notice about the giraffe's song. Ask the learners to turn to the giraffe's song. Ask them to look at the end of each line and to read the last words out aloud. The last word of each line rhymes. Ask the class to read the giraffe's song aloud. Ask them if they could change the rhythm of the song to match the beat of the drum, so that it sounds like a rap. Some learners could keep the beat while others rap the words.

Ask the learners in their groups to read the play again.

4 Read the end of the story to the learners. Ask them to discuss and answer the questions.

Answers
a They do not look alike. A rhino is a huge, heavy, thick-skinned animal with two horns on its nose. A hippo has small ears, a wide mouth and very thick skin.
b Hippos eat grass and shoots.
c There were many rhinos on Earth before there were humans.
d He thinks he is hippo because he has never met anyone that looks like him.
e No, the rhino does not know what a giraffe is.
f A giraffe is very tall. They run in a strange manner, they have a very long tongue and they have to spread their legs far apart to drink water.
g Giraffes like to eat acacia leaves.
h beast: animal; unfurled: unrolled; dejected: unhappy

Workbook page 40
Vocabulary
1 Ask the learners to read the playscript about the baby rhino again. They must find the names of six animals that the rhino met in the word snake. It may be necessary to remind the learners to look at the beginning of the play where the setting and characters are discussed to help them to find the answers.

2 The learners complete the words from the text. They match them to the clues.

Answers
1 hippo, giraffe, meerkat, owl, leopard, monkey
2 human being, ambles, spread, tongue, snuffle, hippo

Student's Book pages 69–70
Grammar
Revise nouns and adjectives. A noun is the name of an object, person or place. An adjective describes (tells you more) a noun. Do a few examples with the learners:

- strange animal: 'strange' is the adjective, 'animal' is the noun
- acacia leaves: 'acacia' is the adjective, 'leaves' is the noun
- cold weather: 'cold' is the adjective, 'weather' is the noun.

Explain that in the previous unit they looked at adverbial phrases. Now they are going to look at noun phrases. A noun phrase is a group of words without a verb. A noun phrase always has a noun and there are usually one or two adjectives that describe the noun.

Example: In the phrase 'an excited baby rhino', 'rhino' is the noun, 'excited baby' is the noun phrase.

1 Ask the learners to copy the noun phrases into their exercise books and to circle the nouns and underline the adjectives.

2 Ask the learners: 'Do the adjectives go before or after the nouns?' (before the nouns)

3 Write these three nouns on the board: 'hippo', 'giraffe', 'legs'. Ask the learners to think about the animals in the play. The learners write their own noun phrases to go with the animal nouns.

Answers
1 funny animals
tasty tufts of grass
freezing cold weather
2 Adjectives go before the nouns.

Writing

Ask the learners to scan the play *Going … Going …* for any words and phrases that describe the giraffe. They should find out what it looks like, how it talks, how it walks and how it drinks water. Make them aware that they may find clues about the characters in the instructions in the play, namely, the words written in italics.

Allow the learners some time to do this. Have a general discussion about their findings.

Explain to the learners that they are going to write a paragraph of 6–7 lines describing the giraffe in the play. In the paragraph they must try to use interesting adjectives and one or two noun phrases.

Workbook page 41

Reading and understanding

Explain to the learners they must complete the sentences to match what they read in the play *Going … Going …* .

Answers
1 his mother was killed by hunters.
2 tasty tufts of grass.
3 giraffe
4 of their height.
5 can almost reach their knees when completely unfurled.

Extension: Ask the learners to write the playscript for the scene in which the baby rhino is captured by human beings and taken to a safe place. Remind them to have a few instructions for the actors.

Student's Book page 70

Grammar

Remind the learners about apostrophes. Your examples from Unit 2 might still be on the display board and could be used as examples. Otherwise revise the use of an apostrophe.

1 Ask the learners to read the sentences from the play aloud. Explain that some of the words have missing letters, because this is the way we speak.

2 The learners write the sentences in their exercise books, but write the words in full.

3–4 Ask the learners to read the next group of sentences aloud. All the words are written in full. Ask how they would say the underlined words when they speak. The learners write down the sentences, using apostrophes.

Answers
2a Well, you are not a hippo.
b I am not?
c That is it.
d You do not know what you are?
e I have never met anyone else like me.
3a you'd
b can't
c you're
d I'm
e She's

Weekly review

Use this rubric to assess learners' progress as they worked through the activities this week.

Level	Reading	Writing	Listening and speaking
■	This group is able to read playscripts aloud but require support to use expression and awareness of different voices. They read and follow some of the instructions to carry out an activity.	This group is able to write a portrait of a character with support.	This group has improved at speaking clearly and confidently in a range of contexts.
●	This group is able to read playscripts aloud with expression and is mostly aware of different voices. They read and follow most of the instructions to carry out an activity.	This group is able to write a portrait of a character with minimal support.	This group speaks clearly and confidently in most contexts.

▲	This group is able to read playscripts aloud with expression and awareness of different voices. They read and follow instructions to carry out an activity.	This group is able to write a clear and accurate portrait of a character with no additional support.	This group speaks clearly and confidently in a wide range of contexts.

Week 3

Student's Book pages 71–74

Workbook pages 42–43

Student's Book pages 71–72

Reading

1–2 Ask the learners to work in groups of three. Explain that they are going to read the play aloud, but not to read the instructions aloud. They may use a drum to make the beat whilst reading the instruction. Tell them to think about the characters whilst they are reading.

When the learners have done this, they read the play aloud again and add movements to help create the characters.

This would be a good opportunity to assess the learners for: improving their performance when reading aloud; reading aloud with expression to engage the listener; reading playscripts with dialogue, with awareness of different voices; adapting movement to create a character in drama.

Writing

1–2 This exercise will be ongoing for the week.

Ask the learners to read silently the instructions and steps in their books.

Discuss the reason for not using speech marks in a playscript. (Speech marks are not used because the actors have not said the words yet/because the actors still have to say the words.)

Read the steps to the learners. When you have finished, ask them to identify the steps. Write the main points on the board:

Step 1: Plan your scene

Who? What? Where? When? How?

Step 2: Draft (write) your scene

Instructions for the actors

Step 3: Read your draft scene aloud

Improve your playscript.

Step 4: Perform your play

Control the amount of time spent on each step, otherwise some pairs will not complete their playscripts. Next to each step that you have written on the board, indicate the time allocated. This will help you to detect and to support those learners who are struggling or getting stuck on a particular step.

Student's Book pages 72–74

Reading

Explain to the learners that they are going to read the poem *The Stone Cutter* silently to familiarise themselves with it in preparation for reading it aloud. After the learners have read the poem ask if there are any unfamiliar words. Ask them to look the words up in their dictionaries.

The learners work with a partner and practise reading *The Stone Cutter* aloud. Remind them to read with rhythm and expression. Focus their attention on the dialogue and the words that are repeated in the poem.

Student's Book page 74

Vocabulary

Ask the learners to look at the sentences from the poem. Discuss which words in each sentence add a lot of meaning to the sentence. Ask: 'What do the words mean?'

Answers

a Then a wild wind blew the cloud away across the sky.
'Wild' tells us that the wind was coming from different directions and that the force of the wind could move a cloud across the sky.
b The wind blew until it smacked into a huge rock.
'Smacked' tells us the force and the sound that the wind made as it hit the rock.
c His hammer went TACK and his chisel went TOCK.
'TACK' and 'TOCK' tell us the sound of the two implements working together. It is also a rhythmic sound, like the ticking of a clock, possibly indicating the length of time for all the wishes to be granted, and the time that it took for the stone cutter to realise that he was the happiest being a poor stone cutter.

d Then he felt a poor stone cutter chipping at his side.

'Chipping' expresses a small action that over time will leave nothing behind.

Workbook pages 42–43

Reading and understanding

1 Ask the learners to write a sentence under each picture to make a summary flow chart of the story of *The Stone Cutter*.

2 Ask the learners to read the questions and to circle the letter of the correct answer.

Answers
a He chipped at the rock. **b** a rich man. **c** It was grander and more powerful than any emperor. **d** The cloud blocked out all the sun's light.

Student's Book page 74

Writing

Explain to the learners that they are going to write a playscript about *The Stone Cutter*. They can use the flow chart from Workbook page 42 as a starting point.

Discuss the characters. How would they speak? What props will the learners need?

Review the steps used for writing the playscript for a scene from *Going … Going …* .

Weekly review

Use this rubric to assess learners' progress as they worked through the activities this week.

Level	Reading	Writing	Listening and speaking
■	This group is able to read plays cripts aloud but require support to use expression and awareness of different voices. They read and follow some of the instructions to carry out an activity.	This group correctly identifies nouns, but requires support to identify and use noun phrases. They use some of the features relevant to the writing of playscripts. They are able to write a portrait of a character with support. They have a basic understanding of the format of a simple playscript.	This group has improved at speaking clearly and confidently in a range of contexts. They listen and remember some of the sequence of instructions. They require support to create a character in drama. They need more time to practise reading out aloud.
●	This group is able to read playscripts aloud with expression and is mostly aware of different voices. They read and follow most of the instructions to carry out an activity.	This group correctly identifies nouns and uses some noun phrases when writing a playscript. They use most of the features relevant to the writing of playscripts and are able to write a portrait of a character. They have a fair understanding of the format of a simple playscript.	This group speaks clearly and confidently in a range of most contexts. They listen and remember most of a sequence of instructions. They are able, with some support, to create a character in drama. There is improvement in reading aloud after being encouraged to practice.
▲	This group is able to read playscripts aloud with expression and awareness of different voices. They read and follow instructions to carry out an activity.	This group correctly identifies and uses noun phrases when writing a playscript. They use features relevant to the writing of playscripts and are able to write a portrait of a character. They have a good understanding of the format of a simple playscript.	This group speaks clearly and confidently in a range of contexts. They listen and remember a sequence of instructions. They adapt movements to create a character in drama. This group practises independently to improve performance when reading aloud.

Unit 8 Amazing ships

Unit overview

The first week is spent reading a non-fiction text. The learners will scan the text to find the answers. Summarising a text is done using a timeline and a fact sheet. Verbs and adjectives are revised. The second week is focused on grammar. The use of commas, suffixes and compound words are explained and practised. At the end of the week, the learners will write a playscript. The third week starts with writing a first-person account. Adverbs and adverbial phrases are revisited. The comprehension exercise is a little different in that the learners need to find information from a labelled diagram, after which they are required to write a description of the vessel.

Reading	Writing	Listening and speaking
3R01 Use effective strategies to tackle blending unfamiliar words to read, including sounding out, separating into syllables, using analogy, identifying known suffixes and prefixes, using context;	3W05 Identify misspelt words in own writing and keep individual spelling logs;	3SL3 Take turns in discussion, building on what others have said;
	3W07 Write simple sentences, dictated by the teacher, from memory;	3SL4 Listen and respond appropriately to others' view and opinions;
	3W08 Write simple playscripts based on reading;	3SL8 Develop sensitivity to ways that others express meaning in their talk and non-verbal communication.
3R02 Read a range of story, poetry, and information books and begin to make links between them;	3W10 Make a record of information drawn from a text, e.g. by completing a chart;	
	3Wa1 Develop descriptions of settings in stories;	
3R07 Use knowledge of punctuation and grammar to read age-appropriate texts with fluency, understanding and expression;	3Wa3 Choose and compare words to strengthen the impact of writing, including noun phrases;	
	3Wa7 Write first-person accounts and descriptions based on observation;	
3R08 Locate information in a non-fiction text using a contents page and index;	3Wp1 Maintain accurate use of capital letters and full stops in showing sentences and check by reading own writing aloud;	
3R09 Uses IT sources to locate simple information;		
3Rw3 Consider ways that information is set out on a page and on a screen, e.g. list charts, bullet points;	3Wp4 Vary sentence openings, e.g. with adverbials;	
	3Wp7 Use question marks, exclamation marks and commas in lists;	
3Rx2 Scan a passage to find specific information and answer questions;	3Wp8 Collect examples of nouns, verbs and adjectives and use the terms appropriately;	
3Ri1 Begin to infer meanings beyond the literal, e.g. about motives and character;	3Wp12 Know irregular forms of common verbs;	
3Ri2 Infer the meaning of unknown words from the context.	3Ws1 Use effective strategies to tackle segmenting unfamiliar words to spell, including segmenting into individual sounds, separating into syllables, using analogy, identifying known suffixes and prefixes, applying known spelling rules, visual memory, mnemonics;	
	3Ws5 Use and spell compound words.	

Related resources

- Audio file: *The Titanic*
- Slideshow 8: Amazing ships
- PCM 15: Comprehension
- PCM 16: Compound word dominoes
- PCM 17: Say, feel, do cards

Introducing the unit

Do some research on big ships through time, including the Titanic. Download pictures of four to five ships or use the slideshow on the digital resource. Make a timeline, vertical or horizontal, and put the pictures of the ships on the timeline with the date that they were wrecked, scrapped or still in use. Some suggestions of the type of ships that you could use on the timeline are an oil tanker, and early sailing ship, a cruise liner, aircraft carrier and an ice breaker ship.

Make a 'fact card' on each ship that you have chosen. Write the name of the ship and a short description on each card. The description should include the length of the ship, how many passengers it could accommodate, the type of ship and any other piece of interesting information. Make a large banner 'Amazing ships'.

Start the lesson by giving the learners the opportunity to view the timeline and the ships. You could also play the soundtrack of the movie *Titanic* during this time. Ask if anyone can share something about the ships. You may need to prompt the learners by asking: 'What is different about each ship? How do these ships move? What were these ships used for?'

Reveal the banner 'Amazing ships'. Explain that the ships on the timeline are all unique in some way. Divide the learners into groups and hand out the fact cards. Ask them to read and discuss the fact cards in their groups. Give each group an opportunity to tell the class an interesting fact about a ship. Help the learners to understand the reason for putting these ships under the banner 'Amazing ships'.

Week 1

Student's Book pages 75–79

Workbook page 44

Student's Book page 75–78

Reading

1 Tell the learners that they are going to read a book about the Titanic. *Again be aware that the story is about a shipwreck and that many people lost their lives when the Titanic sank (some were rescued though), treat the content sympathetically and sensitively, depending on how you think your class may react.* Before the learners start reading, they read the contents page and the index of the book and answer some questions. Ask the learners what they will find on the contents and index pages of a book. (The contents page tells us about the main sections or chapters into which the book is divided. It also gives the page numbers. The index, which is at the back of the book, tells us where to find information about particular ideas or subjects.) Also discuss glossaries, which explain the meanings of words.

Answers
a This book is about the ship *Titanic*, which was the largest ship of its time.
b There are ten chapters or main sections in the book.
c I can read about the *Titanic*'s maiden voyage.
d in the chapter titled: What went wrong?
e Lifeboats appear on pages 12, 13, 16, 19.
f The index is in alphabetical order so we can find the topics we are looking for more quickly and easily.

2 Ask the learners to read the text with a partner. Encourage them to write down unfamiliar words. They must try to work out the meanings of the words from the text.

When the learners have finished reading the text, ask if there were any words that they need explaining. Encourage other learners to help work out the meanings. The learners could also use their dictionaries.

Reading and writing

Ask the learners to scan the text quickly to find the answers to the question. They write their answers in their exercise books.

Answers
a *Titanic* means 'giant'.
b The *Titanic* set sail on 10 April 1912.
c She sailed from Southampton.
d Her destination was New York.
e The ship hit the iceberg at 11:40 p.m.
f It took the ship 2 hours 40 minutes to sink.
g There were not enough lifeboats for all the passengers.

h At least 1,500 people died.
i 705 people were rescued.
j The *Carpathia* rescued the passengers.

Support: Use PCM 15 to check that less able readers can read and make sense of the text. The comprehension questions provide a choice of answers which makes it easier for learners who may be struggling.

Workbook page 44

Writing

Explain a timeline to the learners. (A timeline is a quick way to show events in the correct sequence.) Draw a line on the board. Use a simple example to illustrate how a timeline works.

Ask: 'Did you come to school and then get dressed? Do you have break when you arrive at school or do you first have some lessons?' Ask the learners to put the events in the correct sequence. As they identify the correct sequence, mark it on the timeline. Write the time that they do each particular activity.

Explain that in this activity they are going to draw a timeline to show the voyage of the *Titanic*. First they must read *The Titanic* again.

Answers
10 April The *Titanic* leaves Southampton.
14 April 11:40 p.m. The *Titanic* strikes an iceberg.
15 April 2:20 a.m. The *Titanic* sinks.
15 April 4:00 a.m. The *Carpathia* rescues survivors.
18 April The *Carpathia* arrives in New York with the survivors

Student's Book page 79

Writing

Explain to the learners that they are going to use the information from the text to make up a fact file about the *Titanic*. Encourage them to use the internet to look for more interesting facts about the *Titanic*, such as where it was built, how many cabins there were, how long and heavy it was. When the learners have completed their task, ask them to share an interesting fact that they researched.

Vocabulary

Revise verbs and adjectives. (A verb is an action word, an adjective describes a noun.) Ask the learners to work in pairs. First they identify whether the underlined words are verbs or adjectives. Then the learners find verbs or adjectives that express the same ideas, but in a more powerful or interesting way.

Answers
a saw – verb; touched – verb; poured – verb; big – adjective; cold – adjective; sailed – verb
b saw – spotted; touched – scraped; poured – flooded; big – massive; cold – icy; sailed – raced

Weekly review

Use this rubric to assess learners' progress as they worked through the activities this week.

Level	Reading
■	This group is able to read the contents and index pages and is able, with support, to draw facts from non-fiction texts. They require support to scan texts to find specific information.
●	This group is able to read the contents and index pages and is able to draw facts from non-fiction texts. They are able, with some support, to scan texts to find specific information.
▲	This group is able to read the contents and index pages with understanding and is able to draw facts from non-fiction texts. They are able to scan texts with ease to find specific information.

Week 2

Student's Book pages 80–82

Workbook pages 45–46

Student's Book page 80

Grammar
Ask the learners to read the notepad explanation about commas. Discuss what is meant by 'punctuation'. (Punctuation is using capital letters, commas, exclamation marks, question marks and speech marks.)

1–2 The learners rewrite the sentences correctly in their exercise books. They read each sentence aloud, pausing slightly after each comma.

Answers
1 Mary, Steven, Ali, Valencia and Bongi were all in the classroom.
2 There were chandeliers, beautiful furniture, carpets and a library on the Titanic.
3 There were 20 lifeboats, 1,316 passengers, 913 crew members and some lifejackets on the Titanic.

Workbook page 45

Writing
The learners rewrite the paragraphs with the correct punctuation. Remind them to use capital letters, commas and full stops.

Answers
1 The Titanic was a huge, luxury ship. The first class passengers had beautiful rooms. There were restaurants, a library and a gym in First Class.
2 Mary and her family decided to make a trip to China. She packed jeans, t-shirts, a jacket, underwear and sandals.

Student's Book page 80

Spelling
Revise compound words with the learners. (A compound word is made up using two short words, for example: 'class' + 'room' – 'classroom'; 'lunch' + 'box' – 'lunchbox'.)

Explain to the learners that they are going to make compound words. They may use some words more than once. The learners write the words in their exercise books and learn to spell them.

Answers
iceberg; sealife; seawater; lookout; lifeboat; lifejacket; outlook; shipwreck

Extension Use PCM 16 to develop a game of compound word dominoes. Make a few copies of the sheet and cut out the words. Place the learners in small groups and give each learner a random set of words. Learners then take turns to place a word. The next learner must add a word before or after the word played to make a compound word. Encourage them to have a dictionary at hand to check any words they are not sure of.

Suffixes
Revise suffixes with the learners. (Suffixes are group of letters that you add on to the end of a word or a verb to change the meaning of the word, for example: 'sail' – 'sailor'; 'farm' – 'farmer'.)

Answers
survive – survivor; steam – steamer; freeze – freezer; bake – baker; inspect – inspector; visit – visitor; conduct – conductor; manage – manager; act – actor; photograph – photographer

Workbook pages 45–46

Spelling
1 The learners break up the compound words into single words.

2 Ask the learners to write down nine compound words using the words in the boxes.

Answers
1 every / one; sea / water; no / body; some / where
2 everybody, everywhere, everyone
nowhere, nobody, no-one
somewhere, somebody, someone

Workbook page 46

Vocabulary
The learners circle the word with the most impact in each sentence.

Answers
a terrified; **b** flooded; **c** scrambled; **d** yelled

Student's Book pages 81–82

Writing
1 Refer to Unit 7 when explaining about the playscript. Remind learners that they wrote a playscript about the baby rhino. They are going to imagine that they are on the *Titanic*. Some are passengers and others are people who work on the ship. They have just been told that the ship has hit an iceberg.

Ask the learners to work in groups to discuss the questions.

2 Allow some time for the discussion. Explain that they are going to write a short playscript based on the scene that they have discussed in their groups.

Go over the steps that they should follow:

Step 1: Plan your scene

Who are the characters? Where are they? What will they do? How will they do it?

Step 2: Draft (write) your scene

What will each character say?

Remember to write the instructions for the actors.

Step 3: Read your draft aloud

Make adjustments and improvements to your scene.

Step 4: Perform your play/scene

Speaking

Ask the learners to read the teaching text aloud. Ask them ro think about a time when they watched someone talking on a mobile phone. What did they notice? Was the person happy? Impatient? Angry? What did the person who was talking on the mobile phone do that gave you an idea of how they were reacting? Some possible answers would be: the person was smiling while they were talking, the person was shouting, the person did not talk on the phone for a very long time. Explain that we call this 'body language'.

1 Ask the learners to look at the pictures in their books. Allow them to discuss the questions.

2 Ask the learners to practise and perform the play scene that they have written using body language to show how each character feels.

Weekly review
Use this rubric to assess learners' progress as they worked through the activities this week.

Level	Writing
■	This group is able to write a simple playscript and a first-person account with support. They need support and reminding to use commas and other punctuation correctly. They are mostly able to identify and build compound words.
●	This group is able to write a simple playscript and a first-person account with some support. They have a fair understanding of adverbs, compound words and alphabetical order.
▲	This group is able to write a simple playscript and a first-person account with minimal support. They have a good understanding of adverbs, compound words and alphabetical order.

Week 3

Student's Book pages 82–83

Workbook pages 47–49

Student's Book page 82

Writing

1 Ask the learners to imagine that they were on the *Titanic* and that they survived the accident. They write a short account for a newspaper of what happened to them that night. The learners should use the information from the text *The Titanic*. Explain what is meant by a first-person account. They must write a text as though they are telling a friend what happened. This means that they will use the word 'I' in the text.

The learners look in their books and follow while you read the notepad text. Remind the learners about adverbs and adverbial phrases. (An adverb tells us more about verbs. An adverbial phrase is a group of words that tell us more about verbs.)

2 When the learners have completed their account, ask them to check that they have copied words correctly from the text.

Workbook page 47

Improve your writing

1 The learners identify and underline the adverb or adverbial phrase in each sentence. They rewrite each sentence starting with the adverb or adverbial phrase.

Answers
1 and **2**
a adverb: 'arrived'
Arriving at 4:10 a.m., the *Carpathia* rescued the survivors of the *Titanic*.
b adverb: 'sadly'
Sadly, the *Titanic* had only 20 lifeboats.
c adverbial phrase: 'before it hit an iceberg'
Before she hit an iceberg, the *Titanic* sailed for four days.
d adverb: 'immediately'
Immediately, the *Carpathia* raced towards the *Titanic* to help.
e adverbial phrase: 'on her maiden voyage'
On her maiden voyage, the *Titanic* left England on 10 April.

Extension: Use PCM 17 to classify a set of words or phrases using the headings 'Feel', 'Act', 'Say'. Note that some phrases, such as 'Run quickly', can fit 'act' or 'say'. Let learners sort the words into three categories and then give them time to compare their classification with another learner and discuss any discrepancies.

Student's Book page 83
Reading and speaking
Ask the learners to work in pairs. They look at the picture and read all the labels. Discuss and answer the questions.

Answers
a liquefied natural gas
b This ship has a double hull
c The LNG is stored in tanks in the hull.
d The hull helps to keep the LNG cold and protects the ship against damage.
e The captain is on the bridge of the ship.
f The ballast tank keeps the ship stable and weighs it down in the water.
g Learners' own answers.

Workbook page 48
Writing a description
The learners use the information from the Student's Book page 83 to write a description of an LNG tanker. Remind the learners to check spelling and punctuation.

Student's Book page 83
Vocabulary
The learners put the groups of words in alphabetical order. Ask them to read the notepad text aloud.

Answers
a hull, iceberg, tank, voyage
b captain, chandelier, cold, crew
c scrape, ship, spot, survivor

Workbook page 49
Vocabulary
The learners read the clues to complete the crossword puzzle.

Answers
Across
3 SOS
5 rescued
6 lifeboat
8 hull
Down
1 massive
2 voyage
4 iceberg
7 tilt

Dictionary work
The learners write each group of words in alphabetical order.

Answers
a ballast, boat, button
b eat, elephant, engine
c paint, picture, protect
d Carpathia, Courageous, Queen Mary, Titanic

Weekly review
Use this rubric to assess learners' progress as they worked through the activities this week.

Level	Reading	Writing	Listening and speaking
■	This group is able to use punctuation some of the time to read texts with fluency, understanding and expression. They require support to scan texts	This group need support and reminding to use commas and other punctuation	This group has yet to develop sensitivity to ways that others express meaning in their non-verbal communication. They require support and encouragement to take turns to listen and respond to what

	to find specific information.	correctly.	others have said.
●	This group is able to use punctuation most of the time to read texts with fluency, understanding and expression. They are able, with some support, to scan texts to find specific information.	This group are mostly able to use commas and other punctuation correctly.	This group has developed some sensitivity to ways that others express meaning in their non-verbal communication. They take turns to listen and mostly respond to what others have said.
▲	This group is able to use punctuation to read texts with fluency, understanding and expression. They are able to scan texts with ease to find specific information.	This group are able to use commas and other punctuation correctly.	This group has developed a sensitivity to ways that others express meaning in their non-verbal communication. They take turns to listen and respond to what others have said.

Unit 9 Sights, sounds and feelings

Unit overview

The focus for this unit is poetry. In the first week the learners will look at a limerick, a calligram (shape poem) and an acrostic poem. They will write their own poems and have the opportunity to read them aloud to the class. Two further poems will be discussed and compared, and rhyming patterns will be looked at. Synonyms play an important role in the second week where the learners add verses to a poem using a particular pattern. The learners' listening skills are put to the test at the end of the second week and continuing into the third week, when they are required to listen to four poems. Each poem has a different rhyming pattern; some will appeal to their senses, while others are humorous. Each poem has a corresponding activity which includes adjectives, verbs, compound words and rhyming words. The third week ends with the learners reciting a poem.

Reading	Writing	Listening and speaking
3R01 Use effective strategies to tackle blending unfamiliar words to read, including sounding out, separating into syllables, using analogy, identifying known suffixes and prefixes, using context;	3W07 Write simple sentences, dictated by the teacher, from memory;	3SL1 Speak clearly and confidently in a range of contexts, including longer speaking turns;
3R02 Read a range of story, poetry and information books and begin to make links between them;	3Wa5 Generate synonyms for high frequency words, e.g. 'big', 'little', 'good';	3SL4 Listen and respond appropriately to others' views and opinions;
3R03 Read and comment on different books by the same author;	3Wa9 Write and perform poems, attending to the sound of words;	3SL6 Practise to improve performance when reading aloud.
3R04 Practise learning and reciting poems;	3Wp8 Collect examples of nouns, verbs and adjectives, and use the terms appropriately.	
3R05 Read aloud with expression to engage the listener;		
3R07 Use knowledge of punctuation and grammar to read age-appropriate texts with fluency, understanding and expression;		
3R09 Uses IT sources to locate simple information;		
3Rw1 Consider how choice of words can heighten meaning;		
3Rw2 Consider words that make an impact, e.g. adjectives and powerful verbs;		
3Ri1 Begin to infer meanings beyond the literal, e.g. about motives and character;		
3Ri2 Infer the meaning of unknown words from the context;		
3Rx2 Scan a passage to find specific information and answer questions.		

Related resources

- Audio files: *Ice Cream and Fizzy Lemonade*; *Hurricane*; *I Don't Know What to do Today*; *The Hen*; *Teacher said*; *Riddle*
- Slideshow 9: Sights, sounds and feelings
- Sounds (recording)
- PCM 18: *Riddle*
- PCM 19: Alphabetical babies

Introducing the unit

Have the following ready before starting the unit. Write the words: 'limerick', 'calligram', 'acrostic' on card. Copy the limerick on page 84 of the Student's Book on a large sheet of paper which you will use to demonstrate the format of a limerick.

Interpret the title of the unit, 'Sights, sounds and feelings'. If possible, cover the windows of the classroom, or close the blinds, turn off the lights. Have a recording of different sounds such as: the sound of a storm, waves crashing, ambulance or a fire engine siren, people laughing or cheering or applauding, a bird singing, a baby laughing. The learners enter the classroom and sit down. When they are settled play the audio file.

Ask:

- How did you feel when you walked into the classroom? Why did you feel this way?
- What sounds did you hear? How did the sounds make you feel?
- Which sounds helped you to form a picture in your mind?

Explain to the learners that for the next few weeks, they are going to use their senses. They will use their sense of sight, hearing and feelings (emotions) when reading and listening to poems.

Week 1

Student's Book pages 84–86

Workbook pages 50–51

Student's Book pages 84–85

Reading and speaking

1 Divide the learners into groups and ask them to read aloud the three different types of poems.

2 Discuss the questions.

Ask the learners to read the limerick aloud. Explain that limericks are nonsense poems. They all have the same pattern. Ask the learners to read the pattern of a limerick on the notepad aloud.

The pattern is:

- There are always five lines.
- Lines 1, 2 and 5 have the same number of syllables and they rhyme.
- Lines 3 and 4 have the same number of syllables and they rhyme.

Put up your copy of the limerick and mark the syllables on line 1.

A limerick

Line 1: There / was / a / young / girl / from / Goole, (7 syllables)

Ask the learners to look at the definition of a limerick again. Ask: 'If line 1 has seven syllables, how many syllables will lines 2 and 5 have?' (also seven) Ask the learners to identify the syllables. Show the seven syllables in lines 2 and 5:

Line 2: Who / took / her / pet / snake / to / school.

    It squiggled and wriggled

    And the whole class giggled.

Line 5: Her / teach / er / didn't / think / it / was / cool

Ask the learners to look at the definition of a limerick again. What happens in lines 3 and 4? They have the same number of syllables and they rhyme.

Show the number of syllables in lines 3 and 4, underline the rhyming words. Ask the learners to identify the syllables and rhyming words.

Line 3: It / squig /gled / and / wrig /gled (6 syllables) rhyming word: 'wriggled'

Line 4: And / the / whole / class / gig / gled. (6 syllables) rhyming word: 'giggled'

Workbook page 50

Reading and writing limericks

1 Explain to the learners that they are going to look at a different limerick and divide it up into syllables. They write the number of syllables at the end of each line and circle the words that rhyme.

There / was / a / young / man / from / Ben / gal (8) rhyming words: 'Bengal'

Who /went / to / a / fan / cy / dress / ball. (8) rhyming word: 'ball'

He / thought / he / would / risk / it (6) rhyming words: 'risk it'

And / go / as / a / bis / cuit (6) rhyming word: 'biscuit'

But / a / dog / ate / him / up / at / the / ball. (9) rhyming word: 'ball'

2 The learners write their own limerick.

Extension: Choose a few of the learners' limericks and ask them to copy their work onto card to display in the classroom.

Student's Book pages 84–85

Reading and speaking (continued)

A calligram (shape poem)

Ask the learners to read *Spaghetti* aloud again. Explain that a 'calligram' is shape poem. The words in the poem are arranged in a shape or a picture. Ask the learners to look at the shape of the poem. Do they think it looks like spaghetti? Allow the learners to discuss what they think about the way in which the poem is written. Can they suggest another way?

The learners read the acrostic poem. Explain that an acrostic poem uses the letters of a word or name. Each line of the poem starts with a letter from the name or word.

Display the words 'limerick', 'calligram' and 'acrosti'c on the board. Ask the learners to give a brief definition of each.

Workbook page 51

Writing calligrams

Explain to the learners that they are going to write calligrams in the shapes. They should use interesting words to fit the shapes, they do not have to write full sentences, they can enlarge some words and make others really small. Ask the learners to suggest words that could be used in each shape. Write some of the words on the board as reference for the learners who may find this activity challenging.

For example:

> Clouds: fluffy, float, heavy, brooding, wispy
>
> Umbrella: protect, shade, shower, canopy, drizzle
>
> Phone: chat, ringtone, connect, selfie

Student's Book pages 85–86

Write a poem

1–2 The learners write their own poem. Some learners may find this exercise quite challenging and should work with a partner.

Review the three different types of poems: a limerick, a calligram and an acrostic poem. Ask the learners to read their poems aloud. Display their poems under the relevant headings.

Reading and listening

1 Tell the learners that you are going to read two poems written by Judith Nicholls.

2 Divide the learners into groups. Ask them to compare the poems and discuss the questions.

Answers
2
- Is there a pattern to each poem?
  The poem *Riddle* has short lines with few words.
  In the poem *Teacher said …* all the verses start in the same way, namely 'You can use' and the verses end in the same way, namely '… but don't use SAID!'
- Find examples of words that rhyme.
  Riddle: tail, snail, rocket, pocket, man, can, too, kangaroo
  Teacher said … : muttered, uttered, stuttered, moan, groan, hail, wail
- Find examples of words that have the same beginning sounds.
  Riddle: small, snail
  Teacher said: mumbled, muttered, groaned, grumbled, yell, yodel, grunt, groan, scream, screech
- Are there sentences with the same number of syllables? yes
  Some answers for poem *Riddle*: 'rest-on-a-tail: small as a snail?'
  Some answers for poem *Teacher said …* : 'groaned, grumbled and uttered/professed, droned or stuttered'
- How many sections are there in each poem?
  Riddle: one section

Teacher said ... : three sections
- Which poem did you enjoy most? Why?
Learners' own answers.

Read and discuss the notepads.

Support: Use PCM 18 as an additional activity in which the learners have to look carefully at words and spellings in the poem.

Weekly review
Use this rubric to assess learners' progress as they worked through the activities this week.

Level	Writing	Listening and speaking
■	This group is able to write a limerick and a calligram with support.	This group requires support to speak clearly and confidently. They recite a poem using some expression and have some understanding.
●	This group is mostly able to write a limerick and a calligram.	This group mostly speaks clearly and confidently for longer speaking turns. They recite a poem mostly with expression and understanding.
▲	This group is able to write a limerick and a calligram correctly with no additional support.	This group speaks clearly and confidently for longer speaking turns. They recite a poem with expression and understanding.

Week 2
Student's Book pages 87–90

Workbook pages 52–54

Student's Book page 87
Vocabulary
Ask the learners to read the poem *Riddle* again and answer the questions.

Answers
1 a something that can hop over spaces; **b** runs very fast; **c** its furry skin; **d** a baby kangaroo

2 Ask the learners to work in pairs to read the poem *Teacher said ...* . Explain that one person is going to role-play a word from the box while the other guesses the word. They take turns.

Support: Use PCM 19 to reinforce alphabetical order and to encourage dictionary use. It deals with baby animals, including the joey from the poem.

Student's Book page 87
Grammar and writing
1 The learners work in pairs and read the poem *Teacher said ...* and answer the questions.

2 Ask the learners to think of more synonyms that they could use instead of 'said' and write another verse for the poem. When they have finished give them the opportunity to read their verse to the class.

3 Explain to the learners that they are going to write another verse for the next poem. It will follow the same pattern as the poem *Teacher said ...* . Ask the learners to read the verse aloud. They must think of synonyms for 'walked' and 'laughed' to write their verses.

Answers
1 a rant, yell, bellow, how, cream, screech, shriek, bawl
B mumbled, muttered
2 More synonyms for 'said': thought, whispered, spoke, cried, shouted, replied

Workbook page 52
Writing a poem to a pattern
Ask the learners to suggest words, synonyms, that have the same meaning as 'cried'.

Examples: wept, sobbed, blubbered, howled, wailed, shed tears, shouted, exclaimed, called, yelled, screamed, shrieked, hollered, bellowed

Ask the learners to read the poem *Teacher said ...* aloud. Explain that they are going to write their own poem, but instead of using the word 'said', they are going to use the word 'cried'. Remind them to make sure that the verbs are in the past tense.

Student's Book page 88

Write a riddle

Start the lesson with a few riddles.

For example:

- What has legs but cannot walk? a table
- What has keys, but cannot unlock a door? a keyboard
- What building has the most stories? a library

Explain the meaning of a riddle: it is a verbal puzzle, often with a trick answer.

1 The learners work in pairs and write riddles about an animal that they know. Ask the learners to read the types of clues that they could use.

2 Allow time for the learners to read their riddles to the class.

Student's Book page 89

Listening to and speaking

1–2 Explain to the learners that they are going to listen to some poems. When all the poems have been read, they will discuss and compare the poems. Read the poem *Ice Cream and Fizzy Lemonade*.

Ask:

- Which words describe ice cream? ('sliding', 'soft and cold', 'smooth', 'soothing')
- Which words describe fizzy lemonade? ('bubbles', 'froth', 'rushing', 'pop', 'prickles', 'tickles', 'tingles')
- What is the rhyming pattern? (Lines 2 and 4 rhyme.)
- Which senses does this poem appeal to? (sight, touch, hearing)

Workbook page 52

Reading and understanding

Ask the learners to read the poem *Ice Cream and Fizzy Lemonade* and answer the questions.

Answers
a soft, cold, smooth
b fizzy
c prickles, tickles
d Ice cream is soothing because it is soft and smooth.
e The bubbles in lemonade pop and tingle in your mouth.

Workbook page 53

Vocabulary

The learners complete the chart.

Answers
hearing: lemonade – rushing sound, sudden pop
touch: ice cream – sliding, soft and cold, to the back of your throat
lemonade – prickles and tickles your nose, and tingles the back of your throat

Student's Book page 90

Listening and speaking (continued)

Hurricane

Read the poem *Hurricane* to the learners. Read the notepad feature about Dionne Brand.

Ask:

- Which words tell you what people are doing? ('shut', 'bolt', 'whisper', 'gather', 'pull', 'running')
- In which verse do you know that the hurricane is near? (verse 4) Ask the learners to read this verse aloud.
- Is there a rhyming pattern? (Not really, but in verse 4 all the lines except the last line have words that end with –*ing*.)
- Which senses does this poem appeal to? (sight, hearing, touch)

Workbook pages 53–54

Reading and understanding

Ask the learners to read the poem *Hurricane* and answer the questions.

Answers
1 shut the windows, bolt the doors, gather in the clothesline, pull down the blinds
2 branches falling, raindrops flying, treetops swaying, big wind blowing
3 rain / drop, tree / top
4 Learner's own answers.

Weekly review

Use this rubric to assess learners' progress as they worked through the activities this week.

Level	Reading	Writing
■	This group can practise reciting poems using some expression and punctuation.	This group is able to write a poem to pattern and a riddle with support. They have some knowledge of synonyms.
●	This group can practise reciting poems mostly using expression and punctuation.	This group is mostly able to write a poem to pattern and a riddle. They have a fair knowledge of synonyms.
▲	This group can confidently recite poems using expression and punctuation.	This group is able to write a poem to pattern and a riddle correctly. They have a good knowledge of synonyms.

Week 3

Student's Book pages 89-92
Workbook pages 55–56

Student's Book page 91

Listening and speaking (continued)

I Don't Know What to Do Today

Read the poem *I Don't Know What to Do Today* to the learners.

Ask:

- What type of word is used repeatedly in the poem? Verbs or adjectives or nouns? (verbs and nouns) Ask the learners to give some examples.
- Is there a rhyming pattern? (Yes, every line rhymes.) Ask the learners to give examples of rhyming words.

Workbook page 55

Reading and understanding

Ask the learners to read the poem *I Don't Know What to Do Today* and answer the questions.

1 Match the words that rhyme.

Answers

today – play
TV – tree
bike – hike
head – bed
cat – hat
book – cook
pear – hair
race – face
blue – you

2 The learners complete the next activity. They write a short poem of what they do each day. They use words that rhyme at the ends of the lines.

Student's Book page 91

Listening and speaking (continued)

The Hen

Read the poem *The Hen* to the learners.

Ask:

- Which words describe the hen? ('ferocious', 'pecks', 'flaps', 'insulting', 'bites', 'pursues')
- Is there a rhyming pattern? (Yes, each verse rhymes.) Ask the learners to give examples of rhyming words.

Workbook pages 55–56

Reading and understanding

1–3 Ask the learners to read the poem *The Hen* and complete the activities.

Answers
1   hide – side
      run – one
      eggs – legs
      fowl – howl
      find – mind
      these – knees
2   cry – howl
      fierce – ferocious
      crawl – creep
      chases – pursues
      good – trusty

3 Flow chart order: find a friend, friend hides, on your hands and knees, friend jumps up, you grab the eggs, you run.

4 The learners use the flow chart to write a description of how to get eggs from the hen.

Student's Book pages 89–91

Listening and speaking

Read all four poems again. The learners can follow in their books.

Ask the learners the questions below, and encourage them to use all four poems for their answers.

- All the poems use words that add a lot of meaning to the poem. Give examples from each poem.
- Which poem made you laugh? Why?
- Which poem appealed to your senses (made you feel, smell or hear something)?
- Which poem had the most rhythm? How did the poet create the rhythm?

Student's Book page 92

Grammar

1–3 Ask the learners to write down five interesting words in their exercise books from the poems they have listened to. Identify the words: nouns, adverbs or adjectives. Write a sentence with each verb.

Reading and speaking

Ask the learners to choose the poem they liked best and understood from the ones they have listened to. They learn the poem and recite it with actions.

Read through the tips on performing poems.

Each learner will have the opportunity to recite a poem. Use this activity for assessment.

Weekly review

Use this rubric to assess learners' progress as they worked through the activities this week.

Level	Writing	Listening and speaking
■	This group can identify some, but not all rhyming patterns.	This group requires support to speak clearly and confidently. They recite a poem using some expression and have some understanding.
●	This group can identify most rhyming patterns	This group mostly speaks clearly and confidently for longer speaking turns. They recite a poem mostly with expression and understanding.
▲	This group can easily identify even difficult rhyming patterns.	This group speaks clearly and confidently for longer speaking turns. They recite a poem with expression and understanding.

Formal assessment 3: Units 7–9

Use the test on pages 120–123 to assess how well the learners have managed to cover the objectives from the last three units. Hand out the sheets and let the learners complete them under test conditions. Collect and mark their tests, recording the results in your class record book. Use the mark scheme below.

Total 40

Question 1

Reading (10)

A hearing, sight, touch (3)

B rain (1)

C 'spatter','scatter','clatter', 'splatter' and 'slide', 'glide' (2)

D any two: 'slosh', 'splosh', 'clatter', 'rumble' (2)

E ga / losh (1); um / bre / lla (1)

Question 2

Grammar and vocabulary (15)

A Change the verbs to the past tense. (3)

spotting – spotted

spatter – spattered

jump – jumped

B synonyms (3)

leap – jump

slip – slide

spotting – splatter

C nouns (2)

any two: windowpane / cat / umbrella / barrel / rain / puddle

D Punctuation

The wet cat ran clattering, spattering and sliding into the house. (2)

Capital letter and full stop = 1 mark

Comma = 1 mark

Eve Merriam wrote adult poems, poems for children and picture books. (3)

Capital letter and full stop = 1 mark

Capital letter for Merriam = 1 mark

Comma = 1 mark

E Suffixes (2)

inspect – inspector

build – builder

Question 3
Writing (5)
Correct order (1 mark for each event in the correct order = 5 marks)
- born 20 February 1962 in California
- 1994 Kenn Nesbitt wrote *Scrawny Tawny Skinner*
- was a computer software developer before becoming a poet
- 1998 first collection of poetry was published
- lives in Washington.

Character portrait (10)

1 mark: one paragraph and minimum of 6 lines

1 mark: computer software developer

2 marks: Reason for writing poems: Makes him feel good/happy. Makes the world a happier place.

2 marks: four year old girl (1) who refused to eat dinner (1)

1 mark: 32 years old when he wrote *Tawny Scrawny Skinner*

3 marks: 1–3 spelling and grammar errors

2 marks: 4–6 spelling and grammar errors

1 mark: 7 or more spelling and grammar errors

Stage 3 PCM 1

The Rescue word search

Find and circle the adjectives and nouns below in the word search.

> great   sunny   narrow   soft   edge   gulls
> voice   sheer   anything   blades   harness   belt
> helicopter   waist   ground   friend   face

h	e	l	i	c	o	p	t	e	r
e	v	m	w	a	i	s	t	d	h
s	o	f	t	f	a	c	e	g	a
b	i	w	b	f	s	h	e	e	r
l	c	s	v	e	a	t	g	f	n
a	e	s	g	u	l	l	s	r	e
d	r	u	r	q	n	t	h	i	s
e	l	n	e	b	u	j	p	e	s
s	d	n	a	r	r	o	w	n	i
a	n	y	t	h	i	n	g	d	o
k	a	g	r	o	u	n	d	c	x

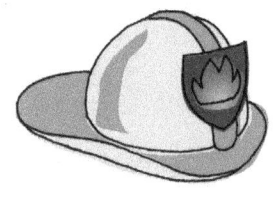

© HarperCollins*Publishers* Ltd. 2016

Stage 3   PCM 2

Book review

Write a book review.

Use the frame below to write a review of a book you've read.

Title: _____

Author: _____

Type of story – tick the boxes:

funny ☐   adventure ☐   scary ☐

traditional ☐   mystery ☐   fairytale ☐

The story is about _____

_____

The bit I liked best was when _____

_____

My favourite character is _____

_____

because _____

_____

Circle a number to show how much you enjoyed the story.

| 1 | 2 | 3 | 4 | 5 |

© HarperCollins*Publishers* Ltd. 2016

Stage 3 PCM 3

Punctuation

1 **Add speech marks and other punctuation to the sentences.**

    a I like walking with my friend   said Tom

    b Help will soon be here   called Alex

    c You must fight to save yourself   said a voice

    d You are lucky to have such a good friend   said Mum

    e I can hear the helicopter   said the rescuer

2 **What would the boys say to each other at the end of the story? Write their words in the bubble.**

© HarperCollins*Publishers* Ltd. 2016

Stage 3 PCM 4

Greetings

What do they say?

Look at each situation.

❶ What do you think the people are saying to each other?

❷ Complete the speech bubbles for each conversation.

Finding facts about germs

Use information books and the internet to find out about germs.

1 Write down six facts that you find interesting.

2 Say where you found each fact.

3 Check each fact is true by finding support in another source.
Say where you checked each fact.

Interesting facts	Source of the fact	Source I used to check the facts

4 Use your facts to prepare a short talk about germs.

Stage 3

PCM 6

Matching pairs

end	finish	start	begin	hurry
rush	choose	pick	sad	unhappy
enjoy	like	smile	grin	shut
close	large	big	small	little
child	youngster	shut	close	sick
unwell	see	look	alike	similar
quickly	speedily	happy	glad	dirty
unclean	quiet	silent	tired	sleepy

© HarperCollins*Publishers* Ltd. 2016

Stage 3　　　　　　　　　　　　　　　　　　　　　　　　　　PCM 7

Hand washing poster

Make a poster to teach about hand washing.

Think about what you have learned and find more information in books or on the Internet if you need it.

1 When should children wash their hands?
Give three different times.

2 How do you wash your hands properly?

Step 1 _____

_____

Step 2 _____

_____

Step 3 _____

_____

Step 4 _____

_____

3 What can happen if you don't wash your hands?
Write three things.

© HarperCollins*Publishers* Ltd. 2016

Stage 3 PCM 8

Judging a book by its cover

Can you judge a book by its cover?

Pick a story book. Answer these questions to help you decide if you'll enjoy it or not.

Title: _____

Author: _____

Look at the pictures on the cover.
Describe what you see.

_____
_____
_____

What sort of story do you think this will be? Tick one or more boxes.

| adventure ☐ | fairytale ☐ | science fiction ☐ | traditional ☐ |
| scary story ☐ | funny story ☐ | sad story ☐ | real life story ☐ |

Write a sentence saying what you think the book will be about.

_____
_____
_____

Does the cover make you want to read the book? Yes ☐ No ☐
Why or why not?

_____
_____
_____

© HarperCollins*Publishers* Ltd. 2016

Stage 3 PCM 9

Cuckoos

❶ Tick the boxes that describe the text you listened to.

poem ☐   story ☐   information ☐

about plants ☐   about animals ☐   about people ☐

facts ☐   opinions ☐   made-up ☐

**❷ Say whether each statement is true or false.
Then provide evidence to support your decision.**

Statement	True or false	Evidence to support your decision.
Cuckoos migrate between Asia and America.		
Cuckoos build their own nests.		
Cuckoos remove eggs from other birds' nests.		
Young cuckoos look after the other baby birds that hatch with them.		
Young cuckoos start their migration in January each year.		

Stage 3 PCM 10

Reading information books

Complete the form for one information book you used to do your research.

Title: _____

Author: _____

Before I read this book, I did not know that:
_____
_____

I learned that:
_____
_____

I also found out that:
_____
_____

The most interesting thing about this book was:
_____
_____

I'd still like to find out more about:
_____
_____

I think I could find more information by:
_____
_____

Stage 3 PCM 11

Australian animals

Here are the names and descriptions of some Australian animals.

> wallaby   platypus   dingo   koala

- Look up the names of these animals in a dictionary or an encyclopaedia or on the internet.
- Write the name of each animal above the description.
- Draw your own picture of each animal.

Wallaby A small- to medium-sized member of the kangaroo family.	
_____ An animal with webbed feet and a bill like a duck. Its body is covered in fur and it has a short tail.	
_____ A 60 cm long animal with short grey fur. It has long claws and looks like a small bear.	
_____ A reddish brown dog-like animal with a bushy tail. It does not bark.	

© HarperCollins*Publishers* Ltd. 2016

Stage 3

PCM 12

What is the question?

Re-read the story of *Tiddalik the Frog*.

Here are the answers to some questions about the story.

Write out the question that you think was asked in each case.

- It got drier and drier and the plants began to die.

- It is set in the outback of Australia.

- The animals tried various things to try and make the frog laugh.

- No, he just sat and watched them.

- Because the eel looked very silly trying to balance on the hot ground.

- It is not good to be greedy. Greed can destroy the plants and animals around us.

© HarperCollins*Publishers* Ltd. 2016

Describing characters

Choose one character that you have read about in this unit.

Write the name of the character and the name of the story the character is from.

Name of character:

_____

Title of story:

_____

Reason I chose this character:

_____

_____

Describe your character.

_____

_____

_____

Write down two questions you would ask if you could speak to the character you chose.

_____

_____

_____

_____

_____

Stage 3

PCM 14

Grammar

1 Circle the correct word to complete each sentence.

   a The world (is/are) coming to an end.

   b Where (is/are) you going?

   c That (is/are) bad news.

   d Where (was/were) you yesterday?

   e She (was/were) at school yesterday.

2 Fill in the blanks with the correct form of the word in brackets.

   a Chicken Licken was _____ a stroll. (take)

   b "I've just met Henny Penny," _____ Cocky Locky (say)

   c I don't want to _____. (die)

   d The friends all _____ into Foxy Loxy's den. (go)

   e Foxy Loxy and his family _____ up every one of them. (eat)

© HarperCollins Publishers Ltd. 2016

Stage 3 PCM 15

Comprehension

Test your comprehension.

1 Circle the correct word in each sentence.

a There were over 2,200 passengers and (crew/lifejackets).

b Late at night the lookout spotted a (lifeboat/iceberg).

c The ship's (lookout/hull) was damaged.

d The *Titanic* began to (tilt/break) and then sank.

e The (crew/survivors) waited in lifeboats.

2 Tick the correct sentence ending.

a The *Titanic* sank because …

- there weren't enough lifeboats on board. ☐
- the ship's hull was damaged by an iceberg. ☐

b There weren't enough lifeboats on board because …

- people didn't think that the Titanic could sink. ☐
- people didn't think they looked nice. ☐

c The shipwreck of the Titanic was found …

- in 1985. ☐
- in 1912. ☐

Stage 3 PCM 16

Compound word dominoes

life	time	less	boat	line	moon
ball	basket	foot	pass	port	able
ice	some	where	no	any	body
ground	super	power	market	less	book
shelf	pipe	light	base	skate	board
key	under	store	keeper	night	house
power	day	speed	ship	town	boat

© HarperCollins Publishers Ltd. 2016

Say, feel, do cards

jump	run	sleep	cry
fall	drown	be quiet	say something
shout	listen	scream	react
sad	scared	terrified	calm
confident	unsafe	nervous	uncomfortable
brave	excited	panic	tired
help!	run quickly	no	don't
it's not fair	bring a rope	I'm worried	come here
yes	I can help	mayday	Where's my sister?

Stage 3 PCM 18

Riddle

Read the poem *Riddle* again.

Find these words.

1 A word that rhymes with tail. _____

2 A word that rhymes with rocket. _____

3 A word that start with *sm* _____ and a word that starts with *sn* _____

4 Words with the letter 'c' that sounds like 'k'. _____

5 Suggest a different title for this poem.

_____

6 Do you like this poem? Give a reason for your answer.

_____

_____

7 Draw and label a picture of a kangaroo with its baby. Use words from poem to help you.

© HarperCollins*Publishers* Ltd. 2016

Alphabetical babies

Read the names of the baby animals in the box.

1 List the baby animals in alphabetical order.

2 Write a short definition of each word.

| chick | kitten | cub | duckling | foal | lamb | joey | calf | tadpole |

Word	Definition
calf	*a young cow*

Stage 3 Formal assessment 1

Formal assessment 1: Units 1–3

Total marks: 45

Read the story and answer the questions.

At the top

Climbers tried and failed to reach the highest peak of Mount Everest for many years. In 1953, a ninth British expedition, led by John Hunt, returned to Nepal. Hunt selected two climbing pairs to attempt to reach the summit. The first pair came within 100 m (330 ft) of the summit on 26 May 1953, but turned back after running into oxygen problems.

Two days later, the expedition made its second and final assault on the summit with its second climbing pair, the New Zealander Edmund Hillary and Tenzing Norgay, a Nepali sherpa climber from Darjeeling, India.

They reached the summit at 11:30 am local time on 29 May 1953. At the time, both acknowledged it as a team effort by the whole expedition. They paused at the summit to take photographs and buried a few sweets and a small cross in the snow before descending.

News of the expedition's success reached London on the morning of Queen Elizabeth II's coronation, 2 June. Returning to Kathmandu a few days later, they discovered that they had been promptly knighted in the Order of the British Empire for the ascent. Tenzing, a Nepali sherpa who was a citizen of India, was granted the George Medal by the United Kingdom. Hillary and Tenzing are also nationally recognized in Nepal, where annual ceremonies in schools and offices celebrate their accomplishment.

(adapted by Lois Lubbe)

Stage 3 Formal assessment 1

Question 1

Reading

A Which word describes the text *At the top*? Fiction or non-fiction? (1)

B What does 'running into oxygen problems' mean? (2)

C Name two things that Hillary and Norgay did at the summit of Mount Everest. (2)

D Why is the 2 June, 1953 significant? (2)

Question 2

Grammar and vocabulary

A Find and write down examples of nouns, verbs, adjectives in the text. Complete the table. (9)

nouns	verbs	adjectives

© HarperCollins*Publishers* Ltd. 2016

Stage 3 Formal assessment 1

B Rewrite the sentence using speech marks. (2)

It took the whole team to get us to the summit answered Edmund Hillary.

_____

_____

C Make four compound words from the words below. (4)

| in | photo | with | some | no | where | graph | body |

_____

_____

D Read *At the top*. Find synonyms for the words below: (3)

attempt _____

last _____

yearly _____

E Write the words in alphabetical order. (1)

cross   summit   oxygen   Edmund   second

_____

F Write the words using an apostrophe. (3)

they had _____

we will _____

were not _____

Question 3

Writing (15)

Imagine that you are Edmund Hillary and have just reached the summit of Mount Everest. Write a short letter to your family describing how you are feeling.

Here are some adjectives that you may want to use.

| amazing | exhausted | elated | proud | tearful |

Stage 3   **Formal assessment 2**

Formal assessment 2 Units 4–6

Total marks: 40

Read the myth and answer the questions

Theseus and the Minotaur

The Minotaur had the body of a man and the head of a bull. It was caged in a vast maze. When the monster was hungry, seven boys and girls were sent into the maze to be eaten alive. A brave young man called Theseus offered to kill the Minotaur. Theseus promised his father that he would put up white sails coming back from Crete, allowing him to know in advance that he was coming back alive. The boat would return with black sails if Theseus was killed.

Theseus met Princess Ariadne, daughter of King Minos, who fell madly in love with him and decided to help Theseus. Princess Ariadne gave a sword and a ball of string to Prince Theseus. "Hide these inside the entrance to the maze. Tomorrow, when you and the other children from Athens enter the labyrinth, wait until the gate is closed, then tie the string to the door. Unroll it as you move through the maze. That way, you can find your way back again. Use the sword to kill the Minotaur," said Princess Ariadne.

Theseus followed her plan and entered the labyrinth with the ball of thread. As he moved through the maze he unravelled the ball of thread. Theseus heard a loud roar and the Minotaur charged. Theseus managed to kill the Minotaur with one stroke of the sword. He escaped from the labyrinth by following the thread.

Theseus took Princess Ariadne with him and left Crete, sailing happily back to Athens.

Glossary

maze/labyrinth a place constructed of or full of intricate passageways and blind alleys.

© HarperCollins*Publishers* Ltd. 2016

Stage 3

Formal assessment 2

Question 1

Reading

A How do you know that this text is a myth? (2)

B Who are the main characters in the story? (2)

C Why did Princess Ariadne help Theseus? (2)

D How did the ball of thread help Theseus? (2)

E What colour sails did Theseus' father see? (1)

© HarperCollins*Publishers* Ltd. 2016

Stage 3 Formal assessment 2

Question 2

Grammar and vocabulary

A Write the plural form. (3)

child _____

this _____

sail _____

B Fill in adverbs or adverbial phrases in the text. (3)

Seven boys and girls were sent _____ to be eaten alive. Theseus promised his father that he was coming back _____. Princess Ariadne said: "Hide these inside the _____."

C Join the two sentences to make a compound sentence. (4)

Theseus heard a loud roar. The Minotaur charged.

_____

_____

You must wait until the gate is closed. Tie the one end of the thread to the door of the labyrinth.

_____

_____

D Use synonyms instead of 'said'. (3)

"I will return," said Theseus to his father. _____

"What colour are the sails?" said the king. _____

"I will kill the Minotaur!" said Theseus. _____

© HarperCollins*Publishers* Ltd. 2016

Stage 3 — **Formal assessment 2**

Question 3

Writing

A Write a simple playscript for the time when Princess Ariadne met Theseus. (12)

Scene 1

A ship arrives in the bay of Crete. Princess Ariadne sees Theseus.

Princess Ariadne: Who _____

_____

_____

Theseus: I have been sent _____

_____

_____

Scene 2

Princess Ariadne meets Theseus before he enters the maze.

Princess Ariadne: I can help you. Use _____

_____

_____

Theseus: _____

_____

_____

Scene 3

Theseus kills the Minotaur and leaves Crete with Princess Ariadne.

Stage 3 Formal assessment 2

B Write down the names of two other myths or legends that you know. (2)

_____

_____

C Using the Dewey decimal classification system, where in the library would you find books on myths and legends? (1)

_____

_____

Stage 3   Formal assessment 3

Formal assessment 3 Units 7–9

Total marks 40

Read the poem at least *twice* before you answer the questions.

> **Weather**
>
> Dot a dot dot dot a dot dot
> Spotting the windowpane.
>
> Spack a spack speck flick a flack fleck
> Freckling the windowpane.
>
> A spatter a scatter a wet cat a clatter
> A splatter a rumble outside.
>
> Umbrella umbrella umbrella umbrella
> Bumbershoot barrel of rain.
>
> Slosh a galosh slosh a galosh
> Slither and slather a glide
>
> A puddle a jump a puddle a jump
> A puddle a jump puddle splosh
>
> A juddle a pump a luddle a dump
> A pudmuddle jump in and slide!
>
> by Eve Merriam

Question 1

Reading

A Which senses does this poem appeal to? (3)

B What specific type of weather is the poem about? (1)

C Write down two rhyming words that end with *er* and two rhyming words that end with *ide*. (2)

© HarperCollins*Publishers* Ltd. 2016

Stage 3 Formal assessment 3

D Write two words that tell you the sounds of the weather. (2)

_____

E Break up the words below into syllables. (2)

galosh _____

umbrella _____

Question 2

Grammar and vocabulary

A Change the verbs to the past tense. (3)

spotting _____

spatter _____

jump _____

B Find synonyms in the poem *Weather* for these words. (3)

leap _____

slip _____

spotting _____

C Find two nouns in the poem *Weather*. (2)

_____

D Rewrite these sentences with the correct punctuation. Use capital letters, commas and full stops. (5)

the wet cat ran clattering spattering and sliding into the house

_____

eve merriam wrote adult poems poems for children and picture books

_____

© HarperCollins*Publishers* Ltd. 2016

Stage 3 **Formal assessment 3**

E Add suffixes to change the verbs into nouns. (2)

inspect _____

build _____

Question 3

Writing

A Use the times, dates and events below to compile a time-line chart about the poet Kenn Nesbitt: (5)

- wrote *Scrawny Tawny Skinner* in 1994
- born 20 February 1962 in California
- 1998 first collection of poetry was published
- lives in Washington
- was a computer software developer before becoming a poet.

_____

_____

_____

_____

Stage 3 **Formal assessment 3**

B Here is some more information about Kenn Nesbitt.

> "I try to write a new poem every week," said Kenn Nesbitt. He puts the poem on his website and waits for children to comment. "I enjoy writing poems because it makes me feel good. When I read a funny poem or hear a funny song it makes me feel happy. I like to make people laugh. I think it makes the world a happier place," responded Kenn. His poems have appeared in magazines, school textbooks, television and on CDs. Kenn was inspired to write a poem after having dinner at a friend's house when a 4-year old girl tried everything she could to get out of eating dinner. "I went home and wrote *Scrawny Tawny Skinner*," said Kenn.

Write a character portrait about the poet. (10)

Write a paragraph of 6–7 lines in which you describe why Kenn Nesbitt writes poems. Try to use interesting adjectives and one or two noun phrases in your paragraph.

Describe

- what he did before
- why he writes poems
- who inspired him to start writing poems
- his age when he wrote his first poem.

_____

_____

_____

_____

_____

_____

_____

Notes

Notes

Notes

© HarperCollins*Publishers* Ltd. 2016

Text acknowledgements

The publishers gratefully acknowledge the permissions granted to reproduce copyright material in the book. Every effort has been made to contact the holders of copyright material, but if any have been inadvertently overlooked, the Publisher will be pleased to make the necessary arrangements at the first opportunity.

HarperCollins*Publishers* Limited for an extract and artwork from *The Rescue* by Alan Durant, illustrated by Steven Jones, text copyright © Alan Durant; for an extract and artwork from *Bugs!* By Sam McBratney, illustrated by Eric Smith, text copyright © Sam McBratney; for cover artwork from *Harry the Clever Spider* by Julia Jarman, illustrated by Charlie Fowkes; for cover artwork from *Africa's Big Three* by Jonathon Scott and Angela Scott; for cover artwork from *Why Can't Humans Fly?* by Sarah Fleming, illustrated by Wes Low; for cover artwork from *Let's Go to Mars!* by Janice Marriott, illustrated by Mark Ruffle; for cover artwork from *The Brave Baby* by Malachy Doyle, illustrated by Richard Johnson; for cover artwork from *Motorcross* by Adrian Bradbury; for cover artwork from *Ella the Superstar* by Ian Whybrow, illustrated by Sam McCullen; for cover artwork from *Fossils* by Dr Andrew Ross; for an extract from *The Journey of Humpback Whales* by Andy Belcher, text copyright © Andy Belcher; for an extract from *Captain Scott: Journey to the South Pole* by Adrian Bradbury, text copyright © Adrian Bradbury; an extract and artwork from *Chicken Licken* by Jeremy Strong, illustrated by Tony Blundell, text copyright © Jeremy Strong; for an extract and artwork from *The Stone Cutter* by Sean Taylor, illustrated by Serena Curmi, text copyright © Sean Taylor; for an extract from *The Titanic* by Anna Claybourne, text copyright © Anna Claybourne. Karen Morrison for Tiddalik the Frog, text copyright © Karen Morrison.

United Agents for an extract from Bookworms by Roger McGough from *All the best: Selected poems of Roger McGough*, published by Puffin (2004); Weather from *Catch a Little Rhyme* by Eve Merriam. Copyright © 1966 Eve Merriam. Copyright renewed 1994. All Rights Renewed and Reserved. Used by permission of Marian Reiner; *At the top*, adapted by Lois Lubbe from an extract from Wikipedia; information about Kenn Nesbitt, adapted from www.poetry4kids.com/blog/biographies. Reproduced by permission of Kenn Nesbitt.

Photo acknowledgements

The publishers wish to thank the following for permission to reproduce photographs. Every effort has been made to trace copyright holders and to obtain their permission for the use of copyright materials. The publishers will gladly receive any information enabling them to rectify any error or omission at the first opportunity.

Cover &p1 Serena Curmi
PCM 15 Denis Burdin/Shutterstock.